Choosing
to
Choose

Intentional Living
is a powerful opportunity
for those who, regardless
of their circumstances,
seek to responsibly enhance
their personal freedom.

Avrom E. King

First Edition – January 1998

Second Edition – March 2000

Library of Congress Control Number 00-090288

Post Office Bin 60130, Phoenix, AZ 85082 USA

Telephone 602-279-5300 • Telefax 602-279-6300

ISBN 0-9678236-0-9

In gratitude and with love,

I dedicate this small book

to my teachers,

Martha Jean King and

Adam Edward King;

and to two dear people

whose spirits always are with me —

my sister, Yvette,

and my mentor,

Dr. Richard M. Weaver

It takes so much to be a full human being. One has to abandon altogether the search for security and reach out with both arms to the risk of living. One has to embrace the world like a lover. One has to accept pain as a condition of existence. One has to count doubt and darkness as the cost of knowing. One needs a will stubborn in conflict but apt always to total acceptance of every consequence of living and dying.

Morris L. West

Contents

Life is occupied in both perpetuating itself and in surpassing itself; if all it does is maintain itself, then living is only not dying.

Simone de Beauvoir

PREFACE TO THE SECOND EDITION

The intended purpose of my book, *Choosing to Choose*, is identified in the Preface to the First Edition. What I wrote in December of 1997 was not wrong. But I now realize that my words and my vision were too narrow and shallow.

The history of this little book is amazing; nearly 3,500 copies were sold without advertising support. Although most of these copies have been mailed to addresses in the USA and Canada, the book has found its way to Japan, China, Australia, New Zealand, Germany, France, Spain, England, Scotland, Ireland and Israel.

This level of acceptance surpassed my expectations. After all — the book would have a limited appeal, I reasoned. It was privately published and thus would not benefit from established channels of distribution. The book was never submitted for review or marketed in any way. Despite these impediments, sales were generated — mostly as the result of the geometric progression of reader recommendations.

We live at a time when it is *not* cool to express enthusiasm. Why, then, has this book been the recipient of the evangelical efforts of so many readers? There is a wonderful synchrony at work here: *Choosing to Choose* is catching the crest of a huge (and hugely important) wave.

There are now hard statistical data which demonstrate that perhaps a third of the adult population of the USA and Canada are diligently seeking a greater measure of autonomy. Often these people cannot readily verbalize their motivations. Their aspirations may be non-verbal or even pre-conscious. But the feelings they're experiencing are strong, and they are searching for a place in the sun that will help them to feel whole, worthy and self-determining. Their desire for autonomy has become an important factor in decision-making, especially those decisions which have quality-of-life consequences. I am reminded of Nathaniel Branden's brilliant insight: "It is difficult for people to act beyond their deepest vision of who and what they believe themselves to be."

This is a fascinating phenomenon. Even when a desire for autonomy is not verbalized, this desire is influencing decision-making in every nook and cranny of our lives. Those who are *not* seekers are being influenced by those who are.

There is another intriguing aspect to what we are witnessing. The desire for autonomy is *not* restricted to the affluent or well-educated. Indeed, there is substantial reason for believing that the individuals who are most influenced by a desire for autonomy often have been modest achievers, educationally and in socio-economic standing.

I first discussed the broad emergence of autonomy as a cultural trend in 1994. A year later I suggested that the magnitude of this trend warranted a special designation. Drawing on the Greek prefix, *meta*, which means "more than" or "greater than", I referred to this trend as a meta-trend. My research strongly suggested that a wide range of apparently unrelated trends would be integrated by the gravitational field of this meta-trend.

For example — it is evident that the extraordinary growth of alternative and complementary health care has been driven by people who are seeking a greater level of personal choice in the determination of their individual health and wellness. We know that this population exceeds fifty million adults and that by every measure, the population is highly diverse. What unifies them is a desire for self-determination.

The "soft" benefits of autonomy are intrinsic to the rapid proliferation of multi-level marketing organizations. The virtual at-home office, the solo consultant and new patterns of employment (shared work is an example) are widely perceived as serving those who want a higher level of personal autonomy. The power of this meta-trend can be easily demonstrated by considering its effects on earlier trends. Compare the feminist movement today with the militant political agendas of 30 years ago. Today's feminist is seeking more than equality; she also wants autonomy.

Of course, technology and opportunity contribute to this meta-trend. But it is remarkably clear that autonomy is the chosen value; technology and opportunity are the available means.

The acceptance of *Choosing to Choose* — particularly the informal, word-of-mouth process by which others have learned of the book — is a related aspect of this meta-trend phenomenon. I am not a shy or reticent person, and I am comfortable in offering my opinion that *Choosing to Choose* has an importance which goes beyond the number of pages or the circumstances of its issuance. It *is* a worthy and meaningful book. But more important than my book is this simple truth: *Living by intent is an idea whose time has come.*

During the past couple of years, I have kept a record of virtually every reader who has commented on the content or context of the book. I've also initiated a few hundred telephone conversations with book buyers. All of this was anecdotal, not scientific. But the opinions I gathered were stimulating and helpful.

From these experiences, I've learned that while my readers value the brevity of the First Edition, they wanted me to place the idea of living by intent within a more comprehensive social context.

A case in point: Several readers of *Choosing to Choose* who are familiar with my work felt that I had seriously erred in not including a discussion of "mental models" in the First Edition. Curing that deficiency was straightforward and fun. But it also put upon me the necessity of preparing the reader for a discussion of "mental models" — and how the idea of "mental models" can be usefully applied to a person's life experiences.

Years ago I shared a studio with a gifted sculptor who worked in wood. Through his carving, often he would discover a flaw in the structure of the wood which required him to re-create the design that he had initially conceptualized. What I remember most is the delight he felt when this happened. Never anger. Not disappointment. He saw the flaw as an unexpected gift.

At the time, I was put off by what seemed to me to be his curious attitude. Today I understand. The preparation of this Second Edition has helped me to honor the ways in which my ideas have sought their own expression. Perhaps that's why nine of the 17 chapters in the Second Edition are entirely new and were specifically written for the book you are now holding in your hands. Material from the First Edition has been significantly revised. The Second Edition is 300 pages compared with 139 pages in the First Edition.

"More" does not mean "better". Here is the editorial standard which I have invoked: If a person who is not familiar with my work chose to read this book, would the exclusion of a specific chapter limit the quality of the reader's experience? That is the question I asked myself and then I would ask it of the several people who were good enough to read my book in manuscript and comment on it.

In a world that loves labels, I am often asked, "What is your book?" The questioner expects a word or phrase in return. "It's philosophy" or "It's cultural history". Many identifying words and phrases have been suggested by my readers. I agree with most of them. But I don't choose to accept any of them.

Let me tell you what *Choosing to Choose* is not. It is not a manifesto; it is not a declaration. It is not a call to action; nor does it offer an action plan. It is not a doctrinal pleading … a political diatribe … or a self-help guide.

My book is an opportunity for a thoughtful person to experience vicariously, with heart and head, a way of life that is simple, direct and profoundly counter-cultural. My fondest hope is that some who read *Choosing to Choose* will *never* be able to expunge the seed of intentional living from their mind; and that other readers will decide, sooner or later, to open themselves to the possibility of this thoroughly natural way of life.

A long time ago I was asked by a man whom I admire to state my life purpose in words that would fit on the back of a matchbook. Here is how I would respond today: *My purpose is to be a positive agent for change in the lives of those who invite me to join with them. I do this by helping these people learn to take better care of themselves.* These few words are my calling, and I feel blessed that I am able to honorably fulfill my calling.

Please permit me a personal note. In recent years I have experienced some painful losses. Because I believe there is meaning and purpose in everything, I have wondered why these losses were given to me. What is their meaning?

I have come to feel deeply that an important reason for me receiving these burdens was to authenticate my message of abundance and intent, and to demonstrate that fear and love cannot co-exist. The message and the messenger were tested in fire and, happily, not found wanting. I know these burdens have made me a more compelling witness and (perhaps) a wiser, more empathic facilitator.

I prayerfully hope that the Second Edition of *Choosing to Choose* will, in ways that I may never know, bring a bit of peace and a glimpse of possibilities to at least some of those who feel trapped by their circumstances.

I continue to feel gratitude for God's grace in my life and the gifts I've received; and for the support that has been given to me.

Avrom E. King
Phoenix, Arizona
December 1999

The real voyage of discovery consists not in seeking new landscapes, but in having new eyes. There is wonderment in the ordinary.

Marcel Proust

PREFACE TO THE FIRST EDITION

This book is intended for three groups of people.

Some are intrigued by the idea of intentional living and they want an overview of what intentionality means and how, if they find it meaningful, they might personally achieve it.

Others have recently subscribed to my LETTER ON INTENTIONAL LIVING, or are considering becoming a subscriber. But as they have read my LETTER, they experienced a bit of a jolt. Rather like walking into a theater during the third act of a five act play. And so they are seeking a sense of context and continuity.

Finally, there are those who respect my work as a futurist and so they have accepted my belief that we are rapidly entering a new era of cosmic proportion. They want to better understand how this will influence their quality of life.

Whatever has put this book in your hands, please know that I hope it will serve you well. I welcome the opportunity to learn from your experience. Your comments, suggestions or criticisms will be respectfully received.

o o o

Several years ago I was chatting informally with a group of clients when someone asked the group, "If each of you could go back to the time of your high school graduation, would you prepare yourself for a different career?"

When it was my time to respond, I said, "Yes. I would earn a doctorate in history and then focus on the study of the history of ideas. Specifically, I would want to explore how the inter-relationship of ideas contributes to the development of culture." (My academic background has been in philosophy, human development and social psychology.)

A man who has known me for a long time looked me in the eye and quietly said, "Well, you may not have a PhD in history. But it seems to me that's exactly what you've been doing for a long, long time."

I knew immediately he was right. I felt a bit silly for having not realized the truth of his observation. But I also felt gratitude and thanks-giving that despite some dark moments, I had been blessed with many opportunities for creating a life of choice and intent.

For the many months this book has been in preparation, I have thought about how this has happened. I have never been overburdened with modesty and so I think I have a realistic sense of my contributions to this outcome. But I also found myself remembering some marker events in my life. Surely my years at the College of the University of Chicago, especially at a time when the genius of Robert Maynard Hutchins was fully flowering, provided me with a foundation that to this day I enormously value. Most especially I thought about an extraordinary man, Dr. Richard M. Weaver, who for seven years was my teacher, my mentor and my friend. Because of where I was (and when), I had the opportunity to participate in several symposia with two magnificent theologians, Reinhold Niebuhr and Paul Tillich. It was Tillich who introduced me to the idea of intentionality as a divine gift.

Over the years, many clients have permitted me to be part of their lives and thereby they were my learning laboratory for the ideas which I'm here discussing. To say "thank you" seems inadequate. But it is heartfelt.

I want to also acknowledge Linda S. Miller whose editorial skills and sensitivity as a writer have contributed importantly to the First Edition of *Choosing to Choose*. Her hand has touched every paragraph. But so softly and deftly, I only know that what I've done has been made better ... even when I cannot specifically identify her influence.

Because I devoutly believe there are no accidents and that nothing is coincidental, I want to also offer a prayer of gratitude for what I believe is God's continuing grace in my life.

Avrom E. King
Phoenix, Arizona
December 1997

Resist what insults your soul.

Walt Whitman

Chapter 1

THE BREAKING OF MY SHELL

Your pain is the breaking of the shell that encloses your understanding. *Kahlil Gibran*

Once upon a time, a long time ago, I started my first *real* job as a "go-fer" and rag-tag assistant to a wonderful man named William. For nearly four years, he was my mentor, friend and taskmaster. Bill was a senior vice president of a large international agency that provided marketing and advertising services to major corporations. I have not seen him in more than 30 years. But I think about him often. I'm sure that at least every month or two, something happens which reminds me of him, and (usually) the recollection brings a smile to my face.

Although I had completed eight years of academic preparation, it was Bill who taught me the difference between an "almost right" and a "precisely right" word. He held to a shocking standard: According to Bill, every product and every service had a "soul" and it was "immoral" to spend a client's money until we had connected with the soul of the product or service.

I was slow to learn what he meant … and even slower in learning how to apply his wisdom. We didn't talk much about this. Bill was a doer more than a teacher. And so he modeled his beliefs. For example, Bill and I would spend many, many days visiting a client's factories … walking the floor … talking to machine operators and even the fellows who delivered raw materials. We spent (Bill would say "invested") hundreds of hours in dialogue with customers … potential customers … past customers … the customers of competitors and those who worked in the distribution channels.

In factory towns the plant manager would usually invite us to have lunch at the country club. But Bill preferred to find the ubiquitous nearby saloon that served hard boiled eggs and fried bologna sandwiches slathered with mayonnaise and slices of onion. He had a compelling desire to talk with people who had hands-on knowledge of what we would be selling, and a bit of heartburn was a small price to pay for the experience.

It's quite remarkable what we learned in these barroom luncheons. I remember him telling me that the only valid way to learn about the business of a company was "from the inside/out and from the bottom/up". It was all of this collected lore that somehow revealed the soul of the product, and it was Bill's prerogative to determine when we were enough connected with the product's soul to write ads or develop a marketing plan.

I did not then appreciate the process. I was impatient. I wanted action. At night I would tell Bill about my conclusions — how we should change the distribution system, where we should advertise, to whom and what we should say. Usually he was amused and he almost always would listen to what I said. Even ask questions. But then he would simply say, "King, express the soul of this product in a single sentence and then we can go home." I sort of understood. But incompletely. As I think back upon this, it was rather like my high school experience with geometry. I sort of understood. But incompletely.

David Packard's management axiom, "management by shuffling around", would not become famous until 1982 when Peters and Waterman wrote *In Search of Excellence*. But nearly 20 years earlier, Bill and I were shuffling around learning about lipstick, tractors, industrial fasteners, seed corn, drugs, health and life insurance, banking, a dozen food products, cross-country trucking, women's support garments, hatchery chicks and perfume.

Once while we were in the field together, our agency lost a big account. Over the next 72 hours, nearly 200 people were fired. I was shaken. "Wow, what an insecure business this is!" Bill responded, "It's only insecure for those who don't carry their security under their hat." He pointed out that while we had lost the account, another agency had gotten it, and most of the unemployed would soon be working with the winning agency, many at a substantial increase in salary.

After I had been with Bill a while, he invited me to go with him to a preliminary meeting with some corporate officers of a *Fortune 200* company who were considering our services. I was thrilled! To me this felt like "big time" stuff. Much more important than trying to dope out the soul of a product. The meeting lasted about two hours. Tentatively, I asked a few questions. My questions were well received and so I asked more questions. After a while I said, "It seems to me that …" and then I verbally offered a definition of the problem and an overview of the solution.

Bill rather abruptly brought the meeting to an end. I didn't know why. I was on a roll, and he was getting in the way. Later, in the elevator, I realized he was angry. He said nothing until our car was out of the parking ramp. Then he quietly told me, "If you ever do this again, you're fired." I didn't understand. "Was my analysis wrong?" His answer: "Probably not." "Was my solution wrong?" His answer: "Perhaps incomplete but probably not wrong."

"Then why are you angry?" I asked. His response was electrifying. "You demeaned our client. You took their dignity. These are bright men and they have spent their lives in this business. You're a punk kid with no experience and after two hours, you're telling them what to do. I'm pretty sure they can stand up to your audacity. But, King, I fear for *your* soul if you think that the consulting business is about defining problems and creating solutions."

Even as I write these words I can feel again how stunned I was. What else is there? There are problems. And there are solutions. What more could there be except problems and solutions? In a remarkably short period of time, I had defined their problem and offered a solution. If there was nothing to solve, then who needs a consultant? Of course,

I argued with Bill. Despite this breach (or maybe because of it), at his invitation we had supper together that night.

Throughout supper he was charming and gracious. Bill fluently read French, Spanish, Latin and Greek ("the gift of a Jesuit education"), and he was an amateur historian with a deep knowledge of the American Civil War and the European Middle Ages. (I still don't understand why his superior mind would choose two such widely separated points of focus.) He talked easily about his family and his interests, and he asked me about my life. I was aware that he had retained a hundred little details from our earlier conversations.

Over cognac, he said: "About today. Here's what's involved. No matter who we are working with, *our light should illuminate the worth of the client.* When that doesn't happen, we lose. Ultimately our soul. That's all there is for me to say. You're a bright fellow. I hope you come to grasp my meaning."

Well, I didn't. Not for a lot of years. But I never forgot what he said and slowly, very slowly, I would catch glimpses of his meaning. Today I consciously strive to keep Bill's dictum at the center of my work.

Since I am reminiscing, I would like to tell you about another mentor. His name was Torkel. While still a graduate student, I needed work. For a while I sold baby furniture door-to-door. Then I became a baby photographer in the basement of a department store. The first job I quit because I couldn't tolerate the winter cold. I was fired from the second job because in the name of creativity (but in violation of company policy) I rearranged the lighting. I saw an ad which asked for a recent journalism school graduate as an apprentice reporter. My total knowledge of journalism consisted of how to read a newspaper. But I created a bogus resume and lied like fury during my interview. I was hired. Torkel was a Linotype operator and the first person I met in the shop. It took him about 11 milli-seconds to discover that I knew nothing about newspapering. He said to me, "I've never met a journalism school graduate who knew much about this business, but you know even less. Did you even go to journalism school?"

I confessed that I had not. He asked me why I wanted the job so badly. I explained my circumstances. He simply said, "I will teach you." That's exactly what he did. I held the job for two years. Received several awards. And Torkel looked upon me with fatherly pride. I was a guest in his home many times. I came to know his wife and two of his three grown children. We talked a lot. He had an eighth grade education and the wisdom of Solomon.

He was awed by the number of years I had been in school. It was not that he didn't value school. His son and daughter (whom I knew) were both college graduates. But it was his belief that "Learning for the sake of learning is an act of ignorance." I didn't agree with Torkel, and I still don't. But then and now, I admire his passionate connection to the question. And surely he was wise when he insisted that in order to have value, learning must somehow benefit people; and that the learner must have a clear sense of altruistic purpose if the learning was to be optimal and honorable.

At this point in my life, I had confused "facts" with "knowledge"; and I was arrogantly invested in helping others to marvel at all the facts I had acquired. The idea that I had an obligation to use what had been given to me for the benefit of others seemed weak and inane. Somehow (in ways that I didn't then grasp), Torkel helped me to see, albeit dimly, the power and beauty of service.

He also taught me about brewing wine and beer, ice fishing, pickling fish and (mostly) having fun. I don't believe I've ever known a person who squeezed more fun out of a day. Any day. Consistently. Day after day. For someone like me, a self-proclaimed stick-in-the-mud, he was truly a tonic.

There are, of course, some enormous differences between Bill and Torkel. But there are some important similarities, too. For example — both men regarded learning as an experience *and in the absence of that experience, both men would question whether learning had really occurred.* In a deep spiritual way, both men contributed to my sense of being, a process that more naturally would have occurred through interactions with my father. For many reasons, this did not happen and so I am enormously grateful that these men touched my life.

How each of us sees work — and our expectations about work — are crucial aspects of our psychological development. When my daughter, Martha, was just seven, I was driving her and a friend to a birthday party. Both girls were intently talking, oblivious to me. Martha said to her friend, "What does your daddy do?" Her friend explained that "He just talks on the phone and uses an adding machine." (In fact, he was a senior vice president of a major bank in Phoenix.) She then asked Martha the same question. Martha said, "All my daddy does is talk on the phone." Despite my education and responsibilities, it took me many years to move beyond the two-dimensional simplicity of work as my young daughter defined it.

Some years later, my son Adam, then age 11, seriously inquired about the work that I do. It was illuminating to explain my work in a way that was honest, relatively complete and understandable to one of his age. Soon after — apparently by coincidence, if you believe in coincidences — a colleague asked some questions about changes she was observing in the way we work with our clients. That started a quite wonderful dialogue which, on and off, had continued for many weeks.

She challenged me to develop our discussion, and to then offer it as a statement of beliefs to my clients. While I've often encouraged my clients to prepare a statement of their beliefs, somehow it seemed a tad awkward and unbecoming for me to take my own advice. In trying to understand my own discomfort, I came to better appreciate the power of this simple exercise. Her suggestion is powerful because she was proposing an act of intimacy which would help you to more fully know who I am. Since I ask you to pay for the privilege of reading my thoughts, you deserve to know me better. Perhaps more important — in your response to *my* beliefs, you will become more clear about *your* beliefs.

The series which follows is neither inclusive nor complete. Remember, please, Goedel's Theorem, a mathematical proof that a system cannot simultaneously be both valid and completed. I think you will quickly see how much I owe to Bill and Torkel.

First — I used to believe that in order to begin a consultation process, it was my obligation to suspend my personal beliefs. Later I decided that suspension was not enough; I needed to be non-judgmental (whatever that means). But now I have come to understand that my beliefs are intrinsically a part of me, and they cannot really be suspended or denied except at dire personal cost. And so today I utilize the methodology of an anthropologist.

Imagine that a group of anthropologists want to study a primitive culture. It would be silly to require them to suspend their own beliefs or, worse, to deny that they had beliefs. Instead — an anthropologist begins with the active assumption that whatever "is" has meaning, and that meaning can only be *appreciated* (not understood, but appreciated) within the context of the overall culture. *Anything which exists had purpose and meaning at its inception; and it still has a purpose and meaning today.*

As a consultant my task is to come to appreciate what "is" without imposing my own expectations or beliefs. "Appreciate" is precisely the right verb. This process involves feelings first, cognition later. It is an integrative process which means, of course, that the process is not merely analytic. Optimally I want to grasp the contextual meaning of what I am seeing. As much as possible I want to see through a client's eyes so that I can better appreciate my client's reality.

My capacity for experiencing a client's reality is catalytic. This is the point at which magic begins! Unless and until I can connect empathically with my client's realities, it's not likely that I can be helpful in any meaningful way.

Second — Shortly after it was published in 1969, I had the good fortune to read a book entitled *Process Consultation*. The author is Dr. Edgar H. Schein. I never met Dr. Schein. But he is one of my heroes, and he has been a guiding light in my own intellectual development.

The idea of process consultation is that the consultant does *not* begin with the definition of a problem; nor does the consultant begin with a series of objectives. The consultant begins by talking to lots and lots of people. As a result of this informal, non-directive communication, a series of objectives is *organically* developed. Then the consultant would ask, "What are the constraints, if any, that might intrude upon this company's ability to achieve these objectives?"

In process consultation a consultant should be less concerned with events and operations, and be more concerned with the *inter-relationship* of events and operations. Schein's approach is dynamic rather than static. He is not bound by an organizational chart; clearly, events and operations cross the boundaries of an organizational chart all the time. Since he is focusing on the dynamics of the relationship of the parts, his work cannot be confined to a specific operation, department or corporate officer. In a word, Schein's sense of process consultation is holistic.

The process consultant understands that different personalities will use the same system in different ways and so they will achieve different consequences. For example, imagine a world-wide manufacturing company which has developed a highly sophisticated computerized system for gathering information about the performance of different plants and their constituent departments. Suppose that this sophisticated system has been demonstrating a deterioration in overall performance of a particular factory. If the chief operating officer is a trusting fellow, he might call the plant manager and say, "I've been noting a fall-off in performance at your factory and I'm wondering what this means to you." In the conversation which follows, the plant manager is able to provide his perspective and then, dialogically, a plan would be developed.

Perhaps the COO would discover that the plant manager had a ready explanation and a plan of action already in mind. ("Our declining performance is related to three factors. One of them will be resolved when we complete installation of the new equipment. By changing suppliers, I believe we've already eliminated a second factor. I'm meeting tomorrow with our operations committee to receive their suggestions about the third factor. Would you like me to forward their recommendations?")

Now imagine that the COO is a distrustful personality. He might choose a more authoritarian, top-down approach which would scrape away the plant manager's autonomy and responsibility. In this circumstance the distrustful COO would ultimately cause the destruction of the sophisticated system for gathering information. Why?

Because in subtle ways, plant managers would begin to alter their input into the system. Garbage in/garbage out. Ultimately the distrustful COO would say, "This sophisticated information-gathering system can't be trusted. Let's abandon it."

Thus, a consultant should focus on the relationship between the parts, not merely the parts. When a consultant begins with objectives and/or problem-solving, he virtually assures that his own work will be static rather than dynamic.

It would be hard for me to overstate the importance of this book to me. It provided what I perceived as a logical, cognitive frame of reference for what my early mentors had known intuitively. I needed a lot of years to learn to become adept in process consultation. But today I cannot imagine functioning in any other mode.

Third — As I started to learn to become a process consultant, I came to realize that what the client specifically defined as "problems" were almost always the *visible* symptoms of ill-defined and unacknowledged constraints.

Without exception and regardless of whether an organization employs five people or five thousand, real problems have human scale. They are not caused by flaws in an organizational chart, internal systems or changes in the marketplace. When I learned to ask "why" enough times, I would always discover that the real problems are within people. How they perceive reality. How they communicate their perceptions. Their fears and their aspirations. Their sense of what is real.

Let me say this another way. Imagine two managers of equal intelligence, experience and education. Imagine that each of them is working in a different industry and at different locales. But both are confronting precisely the same challenges with regard to corporate organization, internal systems and an evolving marketplace. *Their individual response to these challenges — and the leadership which they would provide to their management teams — would reflect their own personal well-being and wholeness.* If as a consultant I am only concerned with outer reality manifestations, which they would no doubt define as "problems", I cannot facilitate change which is both meaningful and enduring. Here's why.

In subtle, powerful and unseen ways, our inner attitudes impose upon us *patterns of expectation and response* that inevitably are more powerful than the structural changes we are able to make in our organizations or systems. Thus, when we work on the outside and alter organizational structure, there may be changes. Perhaps even beneficial changes. But they will not be lasting. Ultimately the inner attitudes of the people will pull them (and their organization) back to the old ways.

An important aspect of my work as a consultant is to help my client become aware of these patterns, what in a later chapter I'll refer to as "mental models", and to understand the circumstances which first caused the development of the now repetitive behavior. As my client becomes aware that those original circumstances are no longer valid, the knowledge is empowering. Soon my client is able to dismantle the patterns and, thereby, become free from these now irrelevant bondages.

In the terminology that I favor today, I believe that our outer-reality problems are an extension of inner-reality attitudes. It is imperative to work inside/out, not outside/in. This means, of course, that when the attitudes of a person are not considered, the misperceptions of that person will ultimately become part of any new system or organization — just as they were part of the discarded system. Even when a person has been transferred from a factory in India to a factory in Indiana, the internalized constraints and misperceptions of that person are transferred too; and ultimately these limitations will again be organizationally represented.

Fourth — I now believe that each person has within him/herself the *innate* capacity to meet the challenges of life with integrity and effectiveness. As a consultant, I devoutly believe that everything my client needs to know in order to prosper is already known. My function is to facilitate a process of self-discovery so that a client can freely draw upon inner resources.

What might be termed "personal mastery" is simply a process which permits an individual to legitimately claim the unfettered energy that is within each of us ... and to direct that energy toward personal objectives that will optimally reflect soul and vision. In the presence of visionary leadership, the personal mastery of individuals becomes organizationally transformational. An organization cannot grow in a positive and enduring way unless and until the people within the organization are *first* able to grow.

I also believe that this capacity for personal mastery is a spiritual gift. That's why I am comfortable in saying with confidence that mastery is available to all of us ... and that all of us can draw upon an abundance of energy in realizing for ourselves all that we can be.

Fifth — I believe in a natural process that I summarize as "living by intent". The essence of intentional living involves our innate capacity to organize our life around what gives us joy and satisfaction in the service of others rather than accepting the cultural norm — which requires us to organize our life around the definition and solution of problems.

Intentional living is the opportunity to empower our lives with personally meaningful choices. In this way, we are able to deal with possibilities, which are limitless, rather than the finite range of probabilities.

Sixth — Whether as a workshop facilitator or a consultant, I have come to discover a simple way for me to assess my effectiveness. When I can truly acknowledge that an engagement has been an important learning experience for me, I observe that my client also has been well served. When I am not receiving fulfillment from what I am doing, my efforts are likely providing a minimal benefit to others.

Indeed, I have come to believe that the depth and quality of *my* learning must be on par with my client's; otherwise I suspect that my client has received less than a full measure.

It follows, therefore, that I am blessed in my work because now my clients are also my teachers. Perhaps that's why this Zen proverb has special meaning to me: *Before enlightenment, chopping wood and carrying water. After enlightenment, chopping wood and carrying water.*

There are two ways to be fooled: One is to believe what isn't so, the other is to refuse to believe what is so.

Sören Kierkegaard

Chapter II

INTENTIONAL LIVING:
SOME IMPLICATIONS

I estimate that over the past ten years, I've spent, on average, at least ten hours each week talking one-on-one with individual clients about how the principles and processes of intentional living can be applied to the ordinary events of life. If this is a fair estimate, then during the past decade I've had at least 5,000 hours of direct client experience (not counting workshops and lectures) that have been focused on intentional living.

Because the issues which confront my clients are remarkably similar, years ago I drafted some short written responses to the human circumstances which my clients were sharing with me. The result was a series of issue-centered Brief Comments. These Comments are constantly evolving; there will never be a final and finished draft.

1. *The Four Elements of Intentional Living.*

The idea of "living by intent" is culturally radical but spiritually enhancing. While it's easy to dismiss the idea of intentional living as impractical, I believe you will discover that the more carefully the idea is examined, the more practical it becomes. Consider with me the principles and processes which can lead us toward a life of fun, fulfillment, service and effectiveness.

- *Fun?* Yes, fun! As we come to understand and appreciate the human psyche, we realize that fun in all of its expressions, certainly including satisfaction and pleasure, is central to the life and learning of the infant and young child. Having fun is one of our earliest and most crucial psychological templates. Today we have an enormous body of evidence which demonstrates that those who find fun in all the nooks and crannies of their adult life enjoy a level of productivity *and* a quality of life *and* a tenure of life which go far beyond their more somber companions.

- *Fulfillment?* The wisdom teachings of the past 10,000 years give eloquent witness to this simple proposition: *The purpose of work extends beyond the economic requirements of life.* Through work, each of us has an opportunity to more fully realize the power of our spiritual being, an energy which I believe is freely available to all of us.

- *Service?* Are we human beings with a soul, or spiritual beings with a body? There are some major consequences to how we respond to these questions. Throughout the wisdom writings of all time and all cultures, great thinkers have near-unanimously voted for the second option. I concur. One consequence is a paradox.

What appears most real has form and substance. But what *is* real lacks form and is insubstantial. From this perspective, the real purpose of life activities (certainly including work) is beyond quantification. By any cultural, social, economic or psychological standard, work is a primary life activity. It follows, therefore, that through work we have an opportunity to reach beyond the ordinary economic metabolism of life. *Work helps us to feed our souls and to find enduring meaning in the ordinary events of our lives.* The catalyst for this process is through our service to others. All meaningful work is values-based, mission-driven and spirit-centered; *when we do not perceive our work to be in the service of others, we abort the meaning of work.* Meaningful work is an affirmation of our spiritual reality. In the absence of meaningful work, we are not real. That is, we cannot be complete.

o **Effectiveness?** Yes, yes, yes! When work permits us to more fully realize fun, fulfillment and service, we have access to clarity of vision and energy of spirit which assures effectiveness...creativity...and productivity of gifts, talents and treasure. This is the distilled essence of abundance.

2. An Emerging Definition of Intentional Living.

Intentional living involves each person's latent capacity to purposefully relate to people and activities that generate joy and satisfaction. Thus intentional living involves the daily representation of abundance in the ordinary flow of life.

Intentional living involves a quality of being that is reserved for those who, through their optimal choice-making, create personally meaningful ways to have fun while seeking fulfillment through service to others.

3. A New Organizing Principle.

The essence of intentional living involves the innate capacity *which all of us possess* to organize our lives around what gives us joy and satisfaction rather than accepting the cultural norm which directs to organize our lives around the definition and solution of problems. Implicit in this idea is the ability of each of us to determine the qualities of life which we personally cherish, *and to then methodically move toward the attainment of the qualities of life we have chosen for ourselves.* Our aspirations become the organizing principle of living. *What we do authentically reflects who we are.* Work provides a frame of reference for our attitudes, beliefs and values.

Through intentional living, **Doing** becomes an expression of our **Being**. Our activities authentically reflect the essence of our personality and spirit. "I do what I am" is a pure expression of living by intent. "Here is who I am. These are my beliefs. They are given life and meaning through my work and so my work truly demonstrates the unique reality of who I am." This is the reverse of our cultural expectations in which our identity and our worth **(Being)** are determined by our activities **(Doing)**.

4. A Universal Challenge.

Through our life experiences, this new organizing principle permits us to confront a universal challenge which is so basic that it can be seen in the life experiences of all people throughout the whole of history: *I am what I do VERSUS I do what I am.*

For more than 300 years, our western traditions (social, cultural, religious, economic, political) have been biased in favor of the belief that "I am what I do." This tradition teaches us, subtly and not-so-subtly, that personal identity is derived from *Doing* rather than *Being*. Of course, one consequence of this is that within this tradition, each person's worth and value is derived from activities. *Should those activities cease, then personal worth and value is lost.* Many of us are familiar with how this happens when we are "enjoying" a holiday or recovering from a bit of the flu.

There is another related problem. This western tradition of *Doing* creates a situation of judging and comparison. Consider this: The basis for judging and comparison is always quantitative. We judge and compare based upon aspects of *Doing* which can be added, subtracted, multiplied or divided. And so the focus of our *Doing* shifts from fun and fulfillment, which are *qualities* of life, to how many and how much, which are *quantities* of life.

There *is* another way, and it is reflected in the statement "I do what I am." This statement asserts that my activities can authentically reflect who I am, e.g., my *Being* is demonstrated through my attitudes, beliefs, values and aspirations. In this way, you are able to perceive me as real and genuine, and I am valued for who I am rather than by what I do.

5. Possibilities Rather Than Probabilities.

Clearly, then, the idea of intentional living moves us beyond the gravitational field of fate, chance, circumstance and probability. *Instead, we organize our lives around meaningful choices.* In this way, we are able to deal with possibilities, which are limitless, rather than the finite range of probabilities. The difference between possibilities and probabilities is exquisite and important. *Probabilities tell us what we cannot achieve; they are centered upon risks rather than benefits. But possibilities are expansive, liberating and focused upon potentialities.*

When we choose to calculate probabilities, we engage in an analytic process by which a whole is reduced to its molecular components. More becomes less. But possibilities are additive and even synergistic. The process is integrative. Parts become a whole and the whole has a meaning and purpose which goes beyond the sum of the parts.

I very much admire the distinction offered by Wayne Dyer. Do we count the number of seeds in an apple? Or do we contemplate the number of apples in a seed? At a high level of probability, the first question can be answered with certainty. But the second question is cosmic in its implications; it centers upon what is possible rather than the science of probability.

6. Responsibility for Input or Outcome?

The challenge here is to grasp the subtle but crucial difference between responsibility for input and responsibility for outcome. *It is feasible for me to accept responsibility for the quality of my input. But I cannot do more than this. The outcome of any situation (indeed, the outcome of all situations) is beyond my control.* I cannot control acid rain, nuclear accidents or the trading price of the yen versus the dollar. I cannot control my children or my clients. Quite literally, there is an endless line of people, events and circumstances which I cannot control; and so, therefore, it is not reasonable for me to accept responsibility for these people, events, or circumstances. *But I can learn to take responsibility for myself.*

The process involves accepting four important personal responsibilities: *First, personal responsibility for the purity of my motives. Second, personal responsibility for the integrity of my actions. Third, personal responsibility for telling you (or anyone with whom I'm in relationship) how I feel. And fourth, personal responsibility for telling you what I want.* These four responsibilities comprise the essence of mature relationships. While most of us are aware that we cannot control outcome, often we spend much of our lives striving to accomplish what experience demonstrates is impossible, *and then we punish ourselves for our unavoidable failures.*

7. What is "Learning"?

If you accept that at our core, we are spiritual creatures, it follows that in a formless, insubstantial but real way, each of us is connected with everyone. The first sense of community involves the new-born and mother. From that moment forward, all true learning occurs in relationships. A specific skill can be taught (outside/in) by a textbook or a video cassette. But learning (inside/out) requires a series of interpersonal self-discoveries which, ultimately, must be expressed, received and acknowledged.

True learning, which *always* is manifested in an enduring alteration of behavior, involves this process: First, awareness of new information. Second, discovery that the new information is personally relevant. Third, an opportunity to share our *feelings* about this personally relevant new information. Fourth, an opportunity to use or apply the information. Fifth, an opportunity to explore how we *feel* about that experience. And finally, the opportunity to incorporate the experience and subsequent experiences in what we do (our behaviors).

8. The Issue of Control.

From this perspective of learning, let me now suggest that when we learn about our personal responsibilities, we also become clear about responsibilities which do not belong to us. When I am able to grasp, at a profound level of being, that I cannot accept responsibility for any other person, event or circumstance, I begin to confront some important questions of control.

The issue of control has two aspects. I can be concerned with my own sense of adequacy, competence and worthiness. This aspect of control permits me to say, at least most of the time, "I cannot control the people, events or circumstances which surround me. But that's OK. Because I am OK, I will be OK." My emphasis is on input.

But when I don't have a clear sense that I am OK, I will often seek to control other people and situations. My focus is on outcome, not input. Perhaps subtly and even benevolently. But, nonetheless, I will be striving to control what is outside me, and thereby default on learning to control what is inside of me.

9. Two Life Scenarios.

I observe that as each of us lives the drama of life, the centrality of the issue of control moves us toward one of two scenarios.

SCENARIO OF IMPOTENCE: In this scenario, my life represents an individual expression of my feelings of inadequacy or incompetence. I feel fear and anxiety. These feelings contribute to my sense of being incomplete or that somehow I'm marred or broken. Often I experience feelings of helplessness and hopelessness, and so I may become filled with cynicism and despair.

On the level of *Doing*, I feel inadequate (which becomes guilt); and on the level of *Being*, I feel incomplete, inadequate or sick (a sense of shame). Inevitably, I will develop ways of coping with these feelings. And inevitably these ways involve the assumption of artifactual roles which protect and isolate my pain. I suppress my natural, child-like capacity for the spontaneous expression of intimacy in favor of learned responses. *In this way, I lose my capacity for freely expressing the essence of who I truly am.*

Over the years, I become less real…even to myself. Latent joy is displaced by bitterness. My dreams wither. After a while, I even come to believe that my life is OK. I drift into an acceptance of smothering pseudo-reality which tells me that what I am experiencing is normal. I come to believe that what I have is what life really offers. Despair, cynicism, pessimism and scarcity become my companions…and so even the idea of abundance connotes a certain lack of reality and responsibility.

SCENARIO OF INTENT: I have another choice: the deliberate and methodical decision to live by intent. The more deeply I am able to acknowledge responsibility for the quality of my input, the easier it is for me to recognize that I cannot accept responsibility for outcome — mine or anyone else's. By investing pride in who I am, the purity of my motives and the integrity of my actions, I am able to release my desire to control outcome.

Gradually I am able to say, "I have learned that I cannot accept responsibility for other people, events or circumstances, and so I understand that I cannot control their outcome or mine. But I also know that I am a worthy, deserving and adequate person whose motives are pure and who is acting with integrity. I know that I'll abundantly thrive, regardless of what the future brings." In this scenario, abundance is real and scarcity becomes the painful response of tortured souls.

10. The Consequences of These Scenarios.

Each of these two sets of attitudes can be conceptualized as a series of bipolar scales. Here are some designations which we might apply to both ends of each pairing. The first word in each pair is often acknowledged culturally as a necessary consequence of contemporary living; the second word represents a hoped-for consequence of intentional living. This polarity is eloquent evidence that intentional living is counter-cultural.

- FEARFUL vs LOVING

- UNDESERVING vs WORTHY

- INADEQUATE vs EMPOWERED

- DRIVEN vs FREE

- CONTROLLING vs EXPANSIVE

- CONTROLLED vs SPONTANEOUS

- FRAGMENTED vs WHOLE

- ANALYTIC vs INTEGRATIVE

- IMPOTENT vs EFFECTIVE

- ARTIFACTUAL vs REAL

- ADDICTED vs CHOICE-FILLED

- APATHETIC vs ECSTATIC

- SCARCE vs ABUNDANT

- FLAWED vs FUNCTIONAL

- I AM WHAT I DO vs I DO WHAT I AM

- I'M A SPIRIT WITH A BODY vs I'M A BODY WITH A SPIRIT

11. Some Implications of (Apparent) Opposites.

It's quite impossible to define "hot" without reference to the idea of "cold". How can we explain "up" except by comparing it to "down"; and "right" makes no sense in the absence of "left". A functional understanding of either "good" or "bad" requires us to possess both ideas, and "on" has no meaning until we grasp the principle of "off". Notice also that when I draw a line to define the quality we know as "convex", the same line immediately identifies its opposite, "concave". Or the line which inscribes a circle simultaneously defines what is inside of the line and, as well, what is outside of it.

This is not a word game or a head trick. There is a very important point here. For nearly 400 years, the cultural flow of our technology and science has helped us to see these (and similar) paired opposites as representing two *separate* qualities. But if neither can be defined without conceptually referencing the other, then perhaps they are not separate. Perhaps each of these pairs represent different aspects of the *same* quality.

Now let's similarly consider some qualities of life.

Can we define "successful" without considering the idea of "failure" or "rich" in the absence of "poor"? How about defining the quality of being we know as "happy" apart from being "sad"? Ignore how either of us might choose to define these words and simply focus upon whether any one of them can be understood except in terms of its opposite.

If you agree with me, then it would apparently follow that "success" and "failure", or "rich" and "poor" or "happy" and "sad" *are not separate qualities but, instead, are different aspects of the same quality.* "Who cares?" you might ask. Well, my friends, to use a word once favored by my son, Adam, the difference is "awesome".

When we create a duality ("success/failure"), then automatically we also create a class or a category of people whom we call "successful" and another class or category whom we label "failure"; and by reason of the establishment of the two distinct groups, we imply that the groups are *inherently* separate; and, for this reason, members of each group are *intrinsically* different.

All prejudice is derived from the philosophically corrupt practice of creating a duality out of a unity. The Nazi view of Aryan separateness is what allowed the horrors of the Holocaust just as the perceived separateness of the Afro-American by Caucasian Americans allowed Jim Crow bigotry.

And so we must ask: "Are there any *real* differences in qualities of life?"

12. What's Real About Differences?

"Well," you might ask, "aren't there real differences between people who are 'successful' and people who are not?" Notice how the question develops a sharp edge when I ask, "Aren't there real differences between a Nazi and a Jew?" Yes, there *are* real differences between people who succeed and people who do not; and there are also real differences between a Nazi and a Jew. *But while these differences are real, they are not intrinsic.* They are learned differences ... that is to say, the differences are acquired. When I suggest the differences are not intrinsic, I mean that they do not exist by nature. They are not inherent or latent. And so while it is appropriate to strive to identify and understand these real differences, *it is crucial we understand that the differences are not intrinsic, and so we cannot legitimately establish separate classes or categories to contain them.*

If in our thinking we permit ourselves to believe there are intrinsic attributes which distinguish those who succeed from those who do not, then we create two *separate* categories: Successful people and failures (or Jews and Aryans). Since the categories are separate, the active inference is that the differences between them are intrinsic. Thus, if I am not now successful, I am always doomed to experience failure.

As you can see, this kind of categorical thinking brings us to pessimism, apathy, helplessness and hopelessness. Even if I sometimes see myself as a successful person, this categorical thinking does not permit me to rejoice in my accomplishments. Instead I am inclined to attribute my accomplishments to "luck" or "good fortune". I tell myself that there are intrinsically lucky people and there are other people who intrinsically do not enjoy good fortune. When I see myself as lucky, I cannot acknowledge my own good efforts. And if I perceive myself as unlucky, I become a victim of fate and circumstance.

13. The Transformational Power of Unity.

Transformation of self (and by implication, transformation of any family system or business organization) involves moving beyond dualities, which I believe are *always* false, and toward an appreciation of unity. Let me summarize this argument by asking you to consider the important difference, psychologically and spiritually, between these two statements:

"I AM NOT A SUCCESSFUL PERSON." This statement expresses a false duality and, as an extension, a false categorization. The implication is that there are **intrinsic differences** between people who succeed and people who do not. Moreover, this is an inherently pessimistic statement and it will always lead the believer toward a worldview of scarcity and fear. "I AM A PRISONER OF PROBABILITIES."

"I HAVE NOT YET LEARNED TO MANIFEST SUCCESS IN MY LIFE." This statement expresses the belief that there are **acquired differences** between people who are successful and those who are not, but these differences are not intrinsic and, therefore, not categorical. The differences are learned …and so I am potentially able to manifest success in my life. For these reasons, this statement is inherently optimistic and it will always lead the believer toward a worldview of abundance and love. "ALL THINGS ARE POSSIBLE."

14. Two Principles: Bondage and Autonomy.

Let me now introduce you to two important principles. The Bondage Principle is so named because it inevitably leads to a loss of autonomy and, thereby, a loss of personal freedom. Nonetheless, the Bondage Principle represents a cultural norm. This Principle tells me that *PAST EVENTS x CURRENT HAPPENINGS = MY INEVITABLE FUTURE.*

Of course, past events have already happened and so they are beyond my reach. Even as I think about current happenings, they are quite literally flying into the past. Thus there is a sense in which I have only a very limited ability to influence what is now occurring. The consequence of this Principle is simple and inescapable: My future is largely and unavoidably fixed. It is the product of two forces which are almost entirely beyond my influence. I am held prisoner by my fixed *PAST* and my fleeting *PRESENT.* I am in bondage.

The Autonomy Principle utilizes the same three chronological sets ... but places them in a different order and, thereby, achieves a magnificently different outcome. The Autonomy Principle states that *PAST EVENTS x FUTURE OF CHOICE = CURRENT HAPPENINGS.* According to this Principle, while I cannot change the past, I can learn from it by courageously and imaginatively asking myself what I cherish about the past ... and what I don't like.

Through this process, I can begin to define a future of choice which is represented by more and more of what I value and less and less of what I don't. Then, having defined the qualities of life which are at the core of my future, I am able to ask myself, "If this is my future of choice, then what actions should I now be taking?" The Autonomy Principle is the strategic point of entry by which all of us are able to move toward a life of choice rather than chance and, in this way, become more intentional in our living.

15. Boundary and the Authentic Self.

Now I would like to introduce the concept of boundary, which in this context is an idea that belongs to psychology rather than geography. Of course, we cannot locate boundary on a post-mortem table and we cannot understand it through histological or morphological study. Nonetheless, boundary is real. Indeed, boundary is a crucial developmental and psychological concept which is an extension of what I will here describe as the Authentic Self.

The Authentic Self is your most pure, least distorted sense of yourself. When I refer to your Authentic Self, I am directing you to your highest and finest desire for, and expression of, altruistic service. *And so your Authentic Self is a symbolic representation of the very best you want for yourself.*

Your Authentic Self is an integration and manifestation of your most noble aspirations. In all of these ways, your Authentic Self is the very essence of who you are. On the most profound level, your Authentic Self is a unique and precious expression of your true psychological and spiritual identity. More than any aspect of physical description or personality, your uncontaminated Authentic Self is who you truly are at your core.

Boundary is the outer edge of your Authentic Self. Boundary is how you define where you end and the rest of the world begins. Through the development of your boundary, you have the opportunity to become more clear about the very essence of your identity. *[Essence = Essential]*

Boundary does *not* mean "wall". A wall is something that you might build in order to keep others out. But boundary does not isolate you. Boundary is what permits you to regulate the accessibility of others to your Authentic Self.

Boundary is what allows me to know where I end and (just as important) where you begin. I've suggested that within your boundary is your most pure, least distorted sense of self. Your highest and finest aspirations are within your boundary; what is inside your boundary is incredibly important stuff. The highest act of intimacy which you can offer is an invitation for me to come inside your boundary. Such an invitation is more than intimate. The invitation carries with it your willingness to be vulnerable. And in that vulnerability you give to me the power to cause you great pain.

An important function of boundary is that it permits you to regulate the ingress and egress of those who you want to know intimately. Indeed, in the absence of boundary (or when one's boundary is only weakly developed), intimacy is not possible. Sexual intercourse cannot be an act of psychological intimacy in the absence of a well-developed boundary.

When your boundary is weak, you are gravely limited in the self-esteem which you can generate. A weak boundary permits the precious stuff of your inner reality to flow out and become contaminated. When this happens, your sense of self is limited, even depleted. But when the precious stuff of your inner reality is kept within a well-developed boundary, you know literally, on the cellular level of your being, that you are a worthy and deserving person.

Should your boundary be weak, then you must constantly seek out (or even create) opportunities to have others affirm your worth. But no matter how hard you try, the good feelings which others give you are soon dissipated. And so you must compulsively work at replenishing the good feelings which you want to receive from others. You do that by learning to please them which means, of course, that you must become more committed to what is outside of you than what is inside of you. There is a hole in your soul, and so you cannot fill yourself with good feelings. You may try to plug the hole in your soul with material possessions. But the apparent benefits of ownership are illusionary and you are left with the hole.

It is axiomatic that those who have a poorly developed boundary will also lack self-esteem. And in the absence of self-esteem an individual cries out to maintain what is familiar. Change is frightening. When change does happen, it generates anxiety. Uncertainty. Fear. *And an overwhelming need to preserve the status quo by not being responsive, proactive and accommodating to change.*

A well-developed boundary permits an individual to walk through pain and fear, and find new ways to emotionally prosper. *This is a person whose security is within.* An individual with a poorly developed boundary must seek security on the outside, quite literally requiring others to affirm his/her worth. But in a harsh environment, this person is experiencing events which support a self-perception of unworthiness, while also denying hope.

I remember seeing a bumper sticker which told me that "Happiness is an Inside Job". Yes, there is a flip quality to the statement which detracts from the truth of it. But, in fact, each of us must accept personal responsibility for our own happiness. No one can make me happy; and I cannot give happiness to anyone else. This is easily understood by those with a well-developed boundary. As I think about the people whose lives I admire, it seems to me that they bring to their ordinary day-to-day tasks a sense of adventure. For them there are no ordinary moments. They are excited by the opportunities inherent in *this* moment ... *and so they live their lives filled with optimism.*

These qualities of life are not learned. They are a natural and spontaneous outcome of a well-developed boundary. Those who possess these qualities of life are able to take delight in the service of others.

Psychodynamically, altruism is an outcome of boundary development. So also is integrity. In the absence of a well-developed boundary, those who help others are really serving themselves. They are seeking gratitude, acceptance, affiliation so that they can be affirmed in their own worthiness. They are reeds bending to the winds of circumstance. Probably they are good people. Well-intentioned. Sometimes confused. Often frustrated. But they cannot achieve true integrity. Their denial of reality may not be consciously intended. But conscious or not, it is a purposeful deceit that mars integrity.

16. Boundary, Accessibility and Functionality.

What I am here calling "accessibility" is a crucial concept. Accessibility involves the ways in which I open myself to others…and how I ask others to open themselves to me. It follows, therefore, that through the development of my boundary, I become more clear about my responsibilities. As I discussed earlier, in all of my relationships, I am responsible for the purity of my motives and the integrity of my actions. I am also responsible for telling you how I feel and what I want. However, I am not responsible for how you might choose to respond to me. Nor are any of us responsible for anyone else's outcome.

This is the position of a person who has a well-developed boundary and who, therefore, is comfortable in identifying and honoring his/her Authentic Self. These are the hallmarks of a psychologically mature individual. These attitudes are *functional*; and they lead to functional behaviors. But in the absence of a well-developed boundary, *dysfunctional* attitudes and behaviors inevitably emerge.

"Functional" and "dysfunctional" are descriptive words; they carry no diagnostic or moralistic meaning. Functional attitudes and behaviors *are* functional because they help us to more fully achieve our aspirations. But if our attitudes and behaviors separate us from our aspirations, then our thoughts and actions can appropriately be described as dysfunctional.

17. Dysfunction and the Erosion of Self.

When our boundary is not well developed, each of us is inclined to want to accept responsibility for the other's outcome or happiness. I commit to fixing you…controlling you…protecting you…providing you with the responses and strategies that I believe are in your best interest.

After a while, *my* feelings of adequacy and worth depend on you *not* taking responsibility for yourself. If you did learn to take responsibility for yourself, then you would be rejecting my rescuing behaviors and this would likely cause me to feel abandoned, inadequate and unworthy. *I need to be needed.* And so together we learn to negotiate and maintain a relationship in which I contractually agree to take care of you…and you contractually agree to let me. *Both of us lose our autonomy.* But much more to the point — both of us abandon all meaningful opportunities for growth.

Because you wear a steel collar and an attached chain, you are not free. But I can't lay down my end of the chain, and so I am not free. Neither of us are able to choose. Our relationship becomes a closed system based on necessity and the perpetuation of the *status quo*.

We are both gripped by fear. You are frightened that I won't be there to take care of you. I am frightened that you won't let me. Both of us deny ourselves and each other the opportunity for meaningful growth. We have a co-dependent contract based upon each other's dysfunctional needs.

Our plight is sad, frustrating and difficult. It is an impossible situation because no matter how hard you try or how sincere your effort, you cannot control me or the circumstances which surround us. Nor can I control you or our circumstances. While neither of us can control the other, each of us is too frightened to accept responsibility for controlling ourself.

Moreover, when our boundary is not well-developed, we are confused about our own identity. Because our sense of self is vague, neither of us can be certain that, alone or together, we are OK. You must have my presence and approval if you are to feel OK. When you don't have my presence and approval, you feel anxious. Abandoned. Insecure and flawed (in the sense of "broken" or "inadequate"). And so you create situations in which you barter molecules of your Authentic Self in return for my presence and continuing affirmation. I become addicted to receiving what you give me. The psychological integrity of each of us is dependent upon agents and agencies outside of ourselves. Neither of us have an internalized sense of our own worth. We chronically require external evidence of our internal adequacy.

18. Wants and Needs.

To want to be with people we enjoy is healthy. And to find delight in their approval is also healthy. The question here pivots on the distinction between wants and needs. When I *want* to be with you and to enjoy your affirmations, it involves choice — yours and mine. When both of us have well-developed boundary, each of us can make those choices based on what serves our individual Authentic Selves. But when I *need* you, our relationship is addictive. I do not have a choice. *Living by intent involves choice and desire, not addictive need.*

There is a further distinction between wants and needs. Wants are expansive. They provide us with a broader range of choices. But needs are restrictive. In needs-based relationships, options and choices become more and more limited.

Now here is the nub of it: *Wants-based relationships require well-developed boundaries; needs-based (addictive) relationships cannot exist among people whose boundaries are well-developed.*

It follows, therefore, that the opportunity for meaningful choices (which means the opportunity to live by intent) is an outcome reserved for those who are actively committed to the development of boundary. Conversely, those people whose boundaries are porous cannot move beyond needs-based relationships. And so they cannot make meaningful choices.

19. Attributes of Addiction.

When an individual's behavior conforms with each of the following attributes, we can properly describe the individual as "addicted". First, the behavior has become routinized. It is ever-present, expected and on-going. Second, the behavior has special meaning, perhaps even hidden and esoteric meaning, to the individual. Third, the behavior is profoundly comforting. Fourth, the behavior is chronic. Fifth, the behavior is obsessive in that the individual persists in thinking about the behavior or planning for it. Sixth, the behavior is compulsive. And finally, the behavior is progressive. This means that in the absence of intervention, the behavior will become more and more of an organizing principle in the person's life.

20. "How Happy Do You Want to Be?"

There are just seven words in this question and only one of them has more than one syllable. At least in this sense, the question is simple. I heard Dan Millman, author of the marvelous book, *Way of the Peaceful Warrior,* ask this question in precisely these words. And I admired the process by which his simple question stimulated group members to respond. For an individual who is open to considering a life of intent, this question is important and far-reaching.

Happiness is a *quality* of life and so it cannot be quantified, measured, added, subtracted, multiplied, divided or compared. *But it can be felt.* Many of us have had social and cultural experiences which tell us that happiness is, at best, fleeting. Or that when we are too happy, we are being diverted from the task at hand. Some think that when we are aware of happiness, it's likely excessive and, after all, everyone knows that while recess is fun and school isn't, real learning occurs in a classroom.

Many of us were raised by adults who, through their words and actions, helped us to understand that the price of survival is eternal vigilance. Wariness becomes a way of life. And so we were advised to limit happiness to specific, dedicated occasions which, by reason of precise definition, are isolated and unreal.

Culturally we tend to look upon vacations as unreal and exceptional. A respite from reality. We must spend a long period of time preparing to have one. We earn it by our hard work. We prepare to leave on our vacation with the implied fatalistic attitude that we may never return. Before we leave we must complete all open tasks, even the trivial ones, so if we die in a plane crash, those around us won't come into a home with dusty furniture, a few unpaid bills and some soiled clothes in the hamper. We must do everything that all right-thinking people would do if they had not been irresponsibly enjoying themselves. And so we are exhausted before we leave as evidenced by the cliché, "Are we having fun yet?" A few days before this unreal experience ends, we begin to re-enter reality (or what we know as reality). We call the office. Make lists. Arrange or confirm appointments. Organize ourselves so that we can work longer days in order to "catch up" and otherwise demonstrate that there is a price to be paid for the unreal quality of life we know as "happiness".

21. Inner and Outer Reality.

Of course, this typical perspective of happiness will not admit spontaneity. So "happiness" becomes controlled, regulated or otherwise scheduled. Notice the consequences of this transformation. Earlier I suggested that happiness is an inner *quality* of life which, therefore, cannot be quantified. But when we strive to control, regulate or schedule happiness, *then we are denying its status as an inner quality of life and, instead, happiness becomes part of measurable outer reality.* This confusion is devastating. Perhaps that's why we need to ask, "Are we having fun yet?" or "Let's leave where we are and go somewhere else so that we can have fun!"

Let me illustrate the differences between inner and outer reality by offering you a few comparisons. Effectiveness is *qualitative* aspect of inner reality; it contrasts with efficiency, a measurable and *quantitative* outer reality characteristic. Healing is an inner reality phenomenon; curing is an outer reality process. Inner reality causes us to ask, "Why?" The outer reality questions are, "How, when, where, what?" The notion of "value" is an extension of inner reality; but "cost" belongs to outer reality. Inner reality lacks form and substance; outer reality requires form and substance. Inner reality is personal, perceptual and always uncertain. Outer reality strives for objectivity, facts and certainty. "Possibilities" belong to inner reality. "Probabilities" are in outer reality. Control of input equals inner reality. Control of outcome equals outer reality.

Whatever can be added, subtracted, multiplied, divided, measured or compared is an aspect of outer reality. Whatever *cannot* be added, subtracted, multiplied, divided, measured or compared is within the province of inner reality.

> Outer reality is not "bad" or less worthy or less important than inner reality. But outer reality is different than inner reality. For the purpose of this discussion, there is one crucial lesson to be learned:

> Inner reality provides our guidance system. Inner reality is our North Star. And so all of us have the continuing life challenge of organizing outer reality in ways that will authentically reflect the cherished qualities of our inner life. What we do and how we do it (outer reality) *must* be determined by who we are (the qualities of our inner being). Of course, this is the reverse of the cultural standard in which we are expected to follow the bouncing ball of outer reality circumstances. Culturally we are taught to hope that later in life, perhaps at retirement, we will finally be free to seek and acknowledge our *Being*. It is impossible to calculate the pain caused by this upside-down cultural perception.

Please carefully consider the above paragraph. I believe these words contain a great and enduring truth which is at the very core of intentional living. It is not *my* truth. It is a truth which permeates the wisdom writings of the past ten thousand years. Ideally, it is a truth which we have first learned in our family of origin, by modeling on the behavior of our parents and later through moral teachings. When this happens, it is a truth which we are then able to comfortably model for our children and our grandchildren. If we did not have an opportunity to learn this truth as a child, we can *choose* to learn it as an adult. But it's not required learning. And it is not learning we can acquire except by active choice. When an individual has not chosen to acquire an appreciation for the sanctity of inner reality, it is difficult to respond to Millman's question, "How happy do you want to be?"

22. "Happy" vs "Content".

An oyster is content. The flow of the tides brings an oyster its food and, simultaneously, removes its waste within highly predictable parameters: tidal cycles, temperature, salinity, acidity, etc. But an oyster cannot be "happy" because happiness implies a quality of emotional response which is beyond an oyster's capacity. *Happiness involves choices* and if those choices are real, then happiness also involves both proactivity and intent.

But, sadly, it appears that many of us have come to accept the oyster's *unexamined* assumption that the level of happiness we've historically received is adequate, normal, perhaps even optimal, and probably all there is…at least in this life. Millman's astute question raises the possibility that there may be more. But even this possibility is a bit intimidating to those who sense how emphatically counter-cultural it is.

Consider this: We were born as a fun-seeking organism. Giving and receiving pleasure is central to how children learn, especially during their first five years of life. Yet culturally we are taught that it is selfish, irresponsible and counter-productive to organize our adult lives around pleasure. How very remarkable!

23. "How Good Can You Stand It?"

This was Millman's second question. His first question raises the possibility there may be more. This second question suggests the possibility of much, much more. From my perspective, Millman's second question is crucial to the idea of intentional living. Let me ask you to accept this second question as serious. Not cute or flip. Suppose, just suppose, that there is a way for you to organize your life around people and activities which give you many opportunities to experience fun ... fulfillment ... service ... and effectiveness. If this is possible, then Millman's question *is* serious. And it warrants a serious response. If you choose to reject Millman's question, or to trivialize it, you are rejecting the possibility of living by intent. That would be a horrid loss.

24. Is Happiness a Fundamental Right?

Let me now extend Millman's two questions with a third question of my own: **"DO YOU BELIEVE THAT YOU HAVE A FUNDAMENTAL RIGHT TO BE HAPPY?"**

I am emphasizing the idea of "fundamental right" because I am suggesting that, in fact, happiness *is* a fundamental right. It is *not* a quality of life that must be earned. It is a right which *now* belongs to you. If you agree, then consider the implications.

I am here using inductive logic and constructing an argument derived from what philosophers call "first principles". There are thousands of examples of this in the religious writings of all people. But I will not cite any of these examples because they may raise doctrinal issues that do not belong in this discussion. Often the United States Senate's consideration of nominees for the Supreme Court involves questions of first principle. But I will not use them as examples because they raise political issues that are outside of my discussion. Instead I will refer you to a radical and subversive document written so long ago that it's becoming acceptable, by those who have carefully read it and those who have not. I am referring to America's Declaration of Independence. The primary author of the Declaration of Independence, Thomas Jefferson, was a man well-schooled in first principle reasoning. His primary intellectual adversary was Ben Franklin, a proponent of deductive logic.

The historical record of America's founding is a wide-screen spectacular battle between these two logic systems and their legislative consequences. Thomas Jefferson's argument carried the day and so the Declaration of Independence talks about "certain inalienable rights" which include the often-quoted "life, liberty and the pursuit of happiness". These are *first principle* rights.

The Declaration of Independence assures us that these *are* rights, not privileges. They do not need to be earned. They simply *are*. Every American, and by implication, every human being, possesses these rights as an aspect of *Being* (inner reality) without reference to *Doing* (outer reality). These rights are "inalienable". They can be lost. An example would be incarceration for anti-social behavior. But these rights cannot be bestowed on another person because intrinsically they already are an aspect of you and me and everyone. How curious that the foundational document of this nation refers to the pursuit of happiness as an "inalienable right" and how very, very curious that today when I suggest it's OK to organize one's life around fun, fulfillment, service and effectiveness, my thoughts seem so *alien* from our traditions.

I am purposefully using "inalienable" and "alien" in the same sentence because I want you to consider the root meaning of the word – "separated from". A right which is "inalienable" is so basic that I cannot exist apart from it. And yet the idea of intentional living does strike many people as separate from ("alien") to our cultural history.

25. A Very Practical Question.

The next question is implied by what I have just discussed. Because this question is so very basic, I don't think that's good enough. I want to explicitly ask: *"If you have a fundamental right to become more fully and completely happy, then do you also have a fundamental right to now begin to organize your life in ways that you believe will better assure your happiness?"* Notice, please, that I am asking YOU to consider this question. YOU. Not you as spouse, parent, business person, professional, community leader or team member. YOU as YOU. Do YOU, on the level of *Being*, have the right described in the italicized sentence above? And do YOU now have that right? Before you dismiss my questions as impertinent, selfish, impractical or worse, I challenge you to think deeply about them.

26. Is It "Selfish" to Live by Intent?

I wonder if King George III, upon reading the colonists' Declaration of Independence, looked upon it as an "impertinent, selfish, impractical" statement? Probably so. But the principle here is that each of us must *first* learn to serve self before we can hope to serve others. To say that this is "selfish" is to make a moral judgment about an issue of developmental psychology. The adult's capacity for genuine altruistic service grows out of, and is extended from, the child's capacity to care for self. It is arrogant beyond belief to argue that I can do for you what I cannot do for myself.

Yes, I am able to transfer tactics to you (perhaps masterfully) which I've not yet actualized in my life. But I do so at the cost of my Authentic Self, and I'm asking you to learn from the outside/in when, in fact, all meaningful learning occurs from the inside/out. Those people who master the principles and processes of intentional living have the energy, capacity, desire and opportunity to serve others in ways that their probability-based brothers and sisters cannot imagine! Through the integration of *Being* and *Doing*, I become whole.

27. Transformational Questions.

Privately and silently, please consider two preliminary questions. Your responses to them will help you to assess your own inner clarity. *"Does it follow that you have the right to seek out people and activities which enhance your feelings of fun, fulfillment, service and effectiveness? And second — does it also follow that you have the right to limit your involvement with people and activities that intrude upon these feelings?"*

As you become better able to feed your soul through your responses to these questions, then your process of learning to live by intent will have actively begun. When a consultation client talks with me about life choices, I often find it's useful to ask three simple but extremely powerful questions. Let me separate these questions from the text of this essay so that, if they have meaning for you, you can photocopy the questions and tack them inside a drawer or on a door or place them in your wallet:

> IF I WERE TODAY THE PERSON WHOM I HOPE TO BECOME, HOW WOULD I RESPOND TO THIS SITUATION?

> TWO YEARS FROM TODAY (OR FIVE YEARS OR TEN YEARS), IF THE QUALITIES OF MY LIFE ARE NOT SIGNIFICANTLY BETTER THAN TODAY, HOW WOULD I THEN FEEL?

> AND WHAT SHOULD I NOW BE DOING TO ASSURE THAT I WILL THEN FEEL GREAT ABOUT THE QUALITIES OF MY LIFE?

28. The Abundance of Intentional Living.

Throughout all of our recorded history (there are no exceptions), we have always lived in a world of finite resources. In this sense, scarcity has been an understandable response.

Nomadic tribes realized that animals in the field and fish in the sea were finite resources. Agricultural civilizations soon discovered that the bounty of the earth was limited. Industrial societies have acknowledged that the raw materials of industry are scarce and so, therefore, they must be appropriately managed. And for the past 100 years, marketers have had to acknowledge that despite their inventiveness, all markets have a finite capacity to absorb the flow of products, even products that are consumed.

Now, for the first time in the history of the world, *we confront the extraordinary opportunities of a non-depleteable, infinitely expandable resource.* I am referring to knowledge, which can be here defined as a synthesis of information and wisdom. Our opportunity is without parallel or comparison. Knowledge is a resource which, whenever and however it is used, always creates more of itself. It is truly non-depleteable. And infinitely expandable.

Is it plausible to plan the next five years of your life based upon the possibility that, somehow, your life will be exempt from this paradigm shift? Or is it possible that your conscious, deliberate choice to enhance your personal happiness would be supported by significant world trends?

Consider the magnitude of this moment. To say that it is enormous strikes me as puny and inadequate. Is there a primitive culture anywhere which will not feel the consequences of this moment? Can we find a square mile on Planet Earth which is so remote and barren that it will not be changed by the force of this moment? Is there a social or political or economic system anywhere that will not fundamentally be changed by the intensity of this moment?

Here is what I believe. If you will choose to understand what is now happening, you will be filled with joy and gratitude that you are alive at this wonderful moment. Through this understanding, you will be able to grasp that no matter who you are or what your circumstances, living by intent is both practical and attainable.

29. *Profound Personal Growth.*

In my experience, a decision to move toward a life of intent is much more of an organic process than a specific event. It happens slowly and subtly. The process is nurtured by reading and thinking…often alone and sometimes in the company of like-minded pathseekers. The process involves infiltration of ideas and percolation of responses. At the start of the process, each of us has a broad range of choices; we are inclined to perceive these choices as evidence of our freedom. But over a period of time, which cannot be reckoned or predicted for any individual, the choices gradually fall away. One day, we are able to acknowledge to ourselves that there is no choice. *Then we are truly free.* And then we understand that this slow process is cumulatively transformational. That is what I mean by "profound personal growth". And here is how I define it: Personal growth is "profound" when it literally requires the redefinition of personal objectives, the reordering of personal priorities and the renegotiation of personal relationships. One of the costs of transformational growth is that as it occurs, we are *required* to confront a small set of core issues. Here is how I express them.

- Fear of isolation and abandonment.

- An inner desire for worthiness and esteem.

- Capacity for trust in self and others.

- Competence and, ultimately, mastery.

- Autonomy, which is ultimately expressed in an abiding sense of personal freedom.

- Love – to be the object of others' love…and to love others.

- Intimacy: a capacity to show another person who I truly am … to be confident that I'll be unconditionally accepted by this person…and for both of us to permit our emerging feelings to infiltrate our relationship.

- Control: moving toward a sense of well-being sufficient to allow me to not seek to control the outcome of others; to accept responsibility for my own input and well-being.

How these issues are represented in each of our lives is unique to the individual. But the fact that each of these issues is represented in all of our lives means that all of us have the latent capacity to relate empathically with one another.

30. Creative Utilization of the Past.

Here is an interesting question: Am I able to utilize my habitual patterns of thoughts and expectations as a launching pad for moving toward new opportunities? Or are these long-ago "mental models" an emotional strait-jacket which limit the range of my choices? Here is what I believe.

NEW ASSUMPTIONS GENERATE NEW ATTITUDES. THESE NEW ATTITUDES CREATE NEW POSSIBILITIES WHICH, IN TURN, WARRANT AND SUPPORT NEW BEHAVIORS.

In order to establish a personal trajectory, it's important to have three points on your lifegraph — where you were; where you are; where you want to be. The challenge is to *not* abandon or ignore the past, but to use it creatively in defining a future of choice.

Remember not the former things, neither consider the things of old. Behold I will do a new thing. Now it shall spring forth.

Isaiah 43:19

Chapter III

ABUNDANCE AND THE IDEA
OF INTENTIONAL LIVING

Here is a metaphor for the craziness of our times that is worthy of a Charlie Chaplin burlesque. It's a real-life incident which I am taking verbatim from Michael Crichton's fictional story, *Congo*.

> A new pharmaceutical factory was built in Western Australia. In this factory all the pills came out on a conveyor belt. A worker had to watch the belt and press buttons to sort the pills into separate bins by size and color. An animal psychologist pointed out that it would be simple to teach pigeons to watch the pills and to then peck colored keys for the sorting process. Incredulous factory managers agreed to a test; the pigeons indeed performed reliably, and were duly placed on the assembly line. Then the Royal Society for Prevention of Cruelty to Animals stepped in and put a stop to it, claiming that it represented cruelty to animals. The job was turned back to a human operator for whom it did not, apparently, represent cruelty.

It's probably true that the lives of most of the people you know are filled with idiosyncratic representations of these factory workers ... the managers ... the animal psychologist ... the pigeons ... and the RSPCA. Fate, chance, circumstance and dogma seem to conspire in ways which deny many people an opportunity for directing their lives through optimal choice-making.

That is why I want to explore the meaning of abundance ... the implications and consequences of an abundant worldview ... and how the principles and processes of abundance can be more fully manifested in your life through the practice of what I called "intentional living".

Abundance is a way of life ... a perspective ... an outlook. Indeed, abundance is nothing less than a worldview. It is a process through which each of us is able to see the world and relate to its inhabitants. Abundance is not a technique or a dogma. Abundance is not measurable or in any way quantifiable. Abundance does not involve money or things; it does involve one's attitude toward money and things.

The idea of abundance is at the very core of the disciplines which, according to wisdom-seekers of all ages, best help us to comprehend the nature and meaning of reality: mathematics; the physical and biological sciences; economics, history, psychology, theology and philosophy. Inevitably and without exception, each of these core disciplines and all forms of creative expression must ultimately acknowledge and utilize principles of abundance, or their contrary, principles of scarcity.

Economics is a useful illustration. We are inclined to look upon capitalism as an example of an abundance philosophy. *But, in fact, the doctrine of capitalism is founded upon scarcity.* Consider a toothpaste manufacturer. The total market equals 100%, and my share of the market expands by me taking some of your share away from you. Moreover, capitalism is founded upon the utilization of extractive and finite resources such as oil, gas, coal, lumber, iron ore and the fish in the seas. This contrasts sharply with what later we will identify as the infinitely expanding, non-depleteable resource of the post-industrial era: knowledge.

Let me begin with the idea of abundance. There are three cardinal beliefs that are central to this discussion. Please consider them with me.

- *All the feelings we most dearly cherish and greatly prize are freely and infinitely available.* This is no small point. It is showing us that the feelings which we most want to experience are abundantly available. That's profoundly reassuring. Simple observation demonstrates that all of us deeply crave the same feelings. Love, peace, recognition, worthiness, a desire to learn and to contribute and to enjoy a sense of well-being. These feelings know no bounds of age, gender, politics, race, nationality or time. The universality of these feelings helps us to understand they are natural; they exist within us as an aspect of our human condition, not in response to external factors.

○ The holy writings of the past 10,000 years offer this paradox; it is the second cardinal belief of an abundant worldview: ***The more we give these desired feelings to others, the more of these feelings we have for ourselves.*** Here, of course, is the point of entry for authentic altruism. We serve ourselves through service to others. And it is through this second cardinal belief that the idea of abundance is irrevocably fused to intentional living.

Intentional living involves a determined and methodical commitment to having abundance in one's own life. This commitment is an organizing principle for the choices that each of us are able to make. By our willingness to make these choices, we are exercising the freedom and autonomy which are inherent to intentional living.

Let me say this another way: Each of us is free to choose abundance, and each of us has the autonomous privilege of implementing that choice through our utilization of the processes of intentional living. When we permit ourselves to seek optimal choices, *which are the essence of intentional living*, we demonstrate an exquisite magnitude of autonomy and freedom. It becomes feasible and practical to move toward an abundant worldview because of the processes of intentional living.

○ ***Quantities of life are an outcome of qualities of life.*** This belief is counter-cultural. But anyone can choose to test the belief within his or her own life and, based on that experience, decide whether the belief is valid. "Happy dollars" are generated as a result of our feelings and attitudes, and our capacity to authentically serve others. When we seek quantities of life without having first prepared ourselves attitudinally, we may acquire material wealth, but at a ruinous cost to our aspirations, integrity, relationships and health.

The dynamic representations of these three beliefs in your everyday life is what I mean by intentional living. And so I am here able to say that: *Intentional living involves each person's innate capacity to purposefully become involved with people and activities which generate joy and satisfaction.* It's really that simple. Not easy. But very, very simple.

By asserting that our capacity for intentional living is innate, I am telling you that the principles and processes of intentional living are natural. This means that when we are able to freely choose, we naturally move toward what is pleasing and away from what is not. This is not a profound or original insight.

But it brings to light that most of the time we organize our lives around a popular but contrary cultural imperative — to define and solve problems. Overtly and covertly, we are culturally admonished to spend our lives enduring what is unnatural, and at cost of enjoying what is natural. In an important example of leveling, this cultural imperative is most strongly imposed on those whose potential gifts are the greatest, and violators of this imperative are deemed to be "selfish".

The word needs definition. Selfish refers to those behaviors by which we serve ourselves without regard for (or at cost to) others. Later I will argue that an understanding of any quality requires an appreciation of its opposite. What, then, is the opposite of selfish behavior? To *not* serve myself in deference for others? No! To do this would be a passive and manipulative strategy which diminishes one's integrity, suppresses the pure and free expression of gifts and, therefore, limits an individual's capacity to contribute creatively to the human community. Moreover, this strategy is arrogant. How can I help you if I have not yet learned to take care of myself?

I maintain that the opposite of selfish, so defined, is to serve self — *but through service to others!* This is an absolute requirement of intentional living, and it's why intentional living is a seedbed of altruism. Those who live intentionally are committed to serving themselves — not selfishly but by way of their contribution to the well-being of others. *Intentional living is vision-based, spirit-centered and mission-driven.* Thus, intentional living enhances one's potential for altruistic behavior. Living by intent is socially productive. The human community is well-served by empowered people. As we authentically help others, we help ourselves to become more effective. And so the community gains.

What we call selfishness is a developmental phase by which a young child begins to define interpersonally the psychological notion of boundary. Through this process, the child begins a process of individuation. Altruism is an outcome of robust development of boundary, and authentic altruism requires a vibrant sense of self. Adults who behave selfishly are not morally flawed. Rather, their psychological development was stalled. In age-appropriate ways, their early life experiences did not help them to define their own psychological limits, and as adults their selfish behaviors are distorted attempts at establishing a pale sense of personal identity. Clearly, then, selfishness denies a person the opportunities of intentional living.

Let me also point out that if intentional living is natural, it must also be simple. Simple in the sense of elegant. The more closely we study the world, the easier it is to appreciate that clarity and simplicity are joined. The absence of clarity (confusion) seems to assure the absence of simplicity (complexity). As we become more clear about complex matters, they become simpler.

Here, then, is a useful definition. *Intentional living involves the regular representation of abundance in the ordinary flow of life.* There are four core processes by which an individual is able to implement an abundant worldview; I have defined these processes as having fun, feeling fulfilled, being in the service of others and, thereby, attaining an exceptional level of personal effectiveness. But for the moment, it is enough for us to realize that we share the challenge of creating a life in which these processes are at an everpresent center rather than peripheral and occasional.

Acknowledging these four core processes of intentional living, I offer you this expanded definition: *Intentional living is a quality of being which is reserved for those who, through their optimal choices, create personally meaningful ways to have fun while effectively seeking fulfillment in service to others.*

In his book, Money and the Meaning of Life, Dr. Jacob Needleman reminds us that the idea of literal or metaphorical hell is not part of Hebrew scripture. But there are references to a lower world called Sheol. I admire what Dr. Needleman says:

Here there are no images of raging fire. No cacophonous sounds. No sulfurous fumes. Sheol is simply and solely the place of shadows: dark, weak existence...continually fading, ever-paler life. Sheol is the realm of **diminished being.** It is the condition of human life which proceeds with ever-diminishing human presence.

It is the movement toward absence, the movement away from God. Let me carefully note that one of the central definitions of God that is given in the Old Testament is **conscious presence.** Moses asks God, "What shall I say to the people of Israel? Whom shall I say has sent me with these Commandments?" The answer he receives, as mysterious today as it has ever been: "Say unto the children of Israel, I AM hath sent me unto you."

Sheol, the lower world of the ancient Hebrews, is the condition of ever-increasing distance from I AM, from one's own conscious presence in the midst of life. It is this state of the human psyche that is the most relevant definition of hell. Beyond all social criticism of our era and beyond all the progress and accomplishments we could name, the conditions of our culture more and more favor the diminishing of our being. The technologies, the inventions, the accomplishments we prize — all of them, almost without exception, are prized because they allow us to live and function more and more automatically, without conscious presence, without I AM.

Call to mind the images of hell that have been offered through the ages by the great wisdom teachings of the world. Begin with the most obvious and common symbol, unquenchable fire. It is not hard to understand this to mean torture by one's own desires. A more modern word for this condition is neurosis, a condition in which one is trapped within an endlessly recurring pattern of emotional suffering in which obtaining the apparent object of one's desire serves only to intensify the desire itself.

More recently, and more interestingly, the word *addiction* has been used to describe this pervasive psychological suffering. Exactly as one may become addicted to a narcotic, so we have our addictive cravings for sex, perhaps, or recognition or food or clothes or victory or money or any of the countless other things or experiences that form the object of what we call our emotions.

We need to understand that when the great thinkers of the past warn us about the evils of our desires, they are speaking of this. They are speaking of addiction. No great teacher, not Christ or Moses or Socrates or Buddha, ever condemned desires as such. No, what they have tried to show us is that we are in danger of allowing these desires to define our sense of identity. We fuel these desires with a certain precious psychic energy that is meant to serve a much higher function in our lives. When our energy is mis-directed, desires become cravings, addictions; and there is no better representation of this state of affairs than the image of unquenchable fire.

In his book, Needleman tells us that "*Hell is the state in which we are barred from receiving what we truly want because of the value we give to what we merely desire.*" Those who live in hell suffer "diminished being". Here are some contemporary examples of the effects and consequences of diminished being. Each of these examples is the contrary of abundance...and each is displaced by moving beyond scarcity and evolving a more abundant worldview. Intentional living provides a method by which each of us, as a matter of conscious choice, can reclaim our soul from the pain of today's Sheol.

- Loss of delight in the ordinary moments of life.

- Apathy, ennui and fatigue.

- The feeling that we are controlled by our circumstances, possessions, work and/or the expectations of others, and the related loss of freedom and autonomy.

- A diminished sense of wholeness…the feeling that we are unworthy, inadequate and incomplete.

- An inner belief (sometimes unrealized, often unexpressed and perhaps pre-verbal) that we are without hope or help, and that we cannot become an effective agent in our own behalf. In a word, an everpresent and invasive sense of pessimism.

- Cynicism and distrust.

- A denial of intimacy and the absence of authentic relationships.

- Loneliness.

- A pattern of heroic desire, intermittent effort and dull failure.

- Compensation through passive-aggressive and addictive behaviors.

- Erosion (or suppression) of a desire for excellence, and a related loss of capacity for mastery.

- And so, for all of these reasons, a chronic sense of fear, anxiety and dissatisfaction.

Here is what I believe: *Intentional living is a feasible and inner-directed process by which we are able to move beyond these dank constraints and move toward a vibrant sense of abundant conscious presence.* Because intentional living is natural, it is not necessary for us to learn how to become more free and autonomous. We only need to unlearn the cultural and family-of-origin constraints which now intrude upon our freedom and autonomy.

I must also tell you that I did not create the phrase "intentional living". In 1953, while still a college student, I heard the great Christian theologian, Paul Tillich, talk about how anxiety erodes a person's capacity for what he called "intentionality" — which he regarded as a divine gift. And as a graduate student, I remember a seminar in which he talked about "living by intent". Those words, and the idea that underlies them, have never left me. Through my journey over the years, I've come to acknowledge that the idea of intentional living is at the center of my life and work.

The idea of intentional living is what has given form, substance and energy to my mission: Helping my clients to know that abundance is naturally their birthright and so they are worthy of living by intent; facilitating their personal discovery of what this means within the experiences of their lives; and supporting them in the creation of strategies for implementing their optimal choices. My best hope is that through my work others will come to better feel the miraculous reality of an abundant worldview; and, thereby, they will discover that intentional living is a personally feasible way of choosing to move toward it.

The realness of reality (and the reality of miracles) does not require measurable form and substance. For years I have carried in my head a simple sentence which David Ben Gurion offered to a skeptical journalist: "In order to be a realist, you must believe in miracles." What a short, simple and gorgeous comment!

A "miracle" is the word we assign to an event which generates transcendent feelings when those feelings are independent of the event's supposed cause. For example – at our current state of scientific knowledge, we can explain rather precisely the birth of a baby. Independent of that explanation is the miracle of the mother's transforming feelings. Is the Easter lily any less a miracle than the empty cave? Is the beauty of the Psalms less miraculous than the parting of the Red Sea? What about the power given to us through the discovery of calculus; is that miraculous? Consider your own life and then please read again the first sentence of this paragraph. I believe that each of us is quite literally inundated by miracles, and that is why in our lives there are no ordinary moments.

The more we are able to appreciate David Ben Gurion's comment, the more fully we are living a life of intent. There are endless possibilities for an implosion of miracles within all of us. I dearly want you to feel the reality of intentional living, and to grasp the miraculous implications of that reality. I want you to *feel* those implications and on the level of feelings, to *know* that intentional living is a personally available choice.

T. S. Eliot asked, "Where is the knowledge that is lost in information? Where is the wisdom that is lost in knowledge?" Regardless of where you are in your life journey, you now have a precious, and a *realistic*, opportunity to experience your own wise miracles.

I believe that spirituality is the only reality we have. The paper you are now holding in your hands is composed of molecules ... and the molecules are collections of atoms. But physicists tell us that these atoms are mostly empty space, containing only some small fields of organized energy. We now know experimentally that the behavior of these fields of organized energy can be altered by our thoughts ... which, of course, are also fields of organized energy.

We are beginning to understand that intelligence is within the cell, and that even single-cell bacteria are capable of social behavior based upon what might be described as logic. Certainly we can demonstrate that our thoughts influence our biology...and more recently we have learned that *your* thoughts can influence *my* biology, even when we are widely separated by distance.

If it is true, as many scientists assert, that virtually everything which is real lacks form and substance, and whatever has form and substance is not real, then I am here writing about reality. About the attitudes, beliefs and values which permit us to move beyond our material illusions and to better grasp what is *really* real. I am writing about the reality of miracles and the miracle of reality.

A set of beliefs has emerged from a review of my own writings since 1980, which concern abundance and living by intent. *I want to share these beliefs with you in the hope they will help you to become more clear about your beliefs.* Perhaps it would facilitate your own process of clarification if you were to simply note in the margin whether you agree or disagree with each of these beliefs, and then you could apply a numeric scale to indicate the intensity of your feelings.

I intend for this to be a private exercise. But what a blessing if there are people in your life who can participate with you in this process.

1. I believe many of us are experiencing profound upheaval in our lives. We are enduring a disruption of traditionally established order, and we are sensing a quality of change which, somehow, is deeper and darker than what we remember from earlier times. These changes are unsettling because often they are discontinuous, unpredictable and severe. Worst of all there is an aura of inevitability to what we are experiencing, and so often we feel a loss of autonomy, freedom and personal effectiveness. There has been a narrowing in our range of choices, and it is sometimes difficult to invest energy and confidence in the choices that seem to be available.

2. I believe these circumstances have caused a broad cultural suppression and distortion of an abundant worldview. The result is an insidious apathy and cynicism, and the fostering of reliance on scarcity-derived values.

3. I believe each of us is influenced by an array of family, business, institutional and cultural systems which tend to change only a little even as our

circumstances are changing a lot. Most of the time we act on the belief that these systems are benevolent and effective. Yet we created these systems (or were attracted to them) based upon long-forgotten assumptions, usually derived from a scarcity perspective, which now seem to intrude upon our capacity to achieve a life of choice.

4. I believe that often we are not well served by the underlying attitudes, beliefs and values of these systems. And so the systems which manifest these attitudes, beliefs and values tend to become functionally ineffective and depositories of scarcity. We become so busy tinkering with the systems that there is no time or energy to examine our grievous loss of abundance.

5. I believe individuals can optimally redefine themselves through their relationships, and that this process of redefinition facilitates supportive organizational change. Ultimately, the consequences of this process are transformationally abundant.

6. I believe the questions we dare to ask directly influence the quality of our individual lives. When each of us raises important questions, we are thereby contributing to our own well-being and in this way, we encourage those who are important to us to also ask important questions.

7. I believe that as a result of this process, we learn to establish functional priorities, redefine our objectives and renegotiate the terms and conditions of our relationships. While this process may be scary, it is also creative, productive and spiritually satisfying. Gradually we learn how our Doing Self can authentically reflect our Being Self.

8. I believe this permits us to move beyond the gravitational field of fate, chance and circumstance. We learn to define our choices based upon possibilities (abundance) rather than probabilities (scarcity). And so the idea of living intentionally becomes real and feasible.

9. I believe the possibility of intentional living helps us to perceive our most pure and least distorted sense of self, and it is this sense of idealized self which gives us our opportunity to define who we truly are and, thereby, how we can best relate to others in a benevolent and abundant universe.

10. I believe this evolving sense of personal boundary helps us to learn about effective, wants-based relationships. Through these relationships, we learn to create systems that serve us.

11. I believe these functional systems facilitate our perception of cosmic and transcendent opportunities for service.

12. I believe this cosmic, transcendental perspective is most clear when we view time on a millennium scale of a thousand years, and that the cultural meta-trends which then become visible are instructive and promising.

13. I believe there is significant evidence that the processes and principles of living by intent are both physiologically and psychologically beneficial.

14. As we move toward intentional living, I believe the ultimate strategic question is: *If I were today the person whom I hope to become, how would I now respond to the situation which I'm confronting?*

15. I believe optimism is, potentially, the most beneficial attitude available to us and that pessimism is the most devastating. Our innate optimism/pessimism determines how we perceive the world and the people in it, and how we see ourselves in relationship to the world and its inhabitants. Optimism and pessimism have more (and quicker) impact on our physical, cognitive, emotional and spiritual well-being than any other attitudes. These attitudes directly influence our capacity for giving and receiving love, accepting and providing intimacy and they are primary determinants of how we perceive our own intrinsic sense of worthiness.

16. I believe that optimism is natural and that pessimism is learned. What's been learned can be unlearned, and the best way for this to happen is to displace the old perception with a new attitude that is more soul-satisfying.

17. I believe that optimism is fused to abundance; while pessimism inevitably generates scarcity.

18. I believe we choose, consciously or not, to live within one of two energy fields. The first is defined by optimism, abundance and love; the other by pessimism, scarcity and fear.

19. I believe the events in our lives are selected and defined by the energy we emit and receive. And the quality of the energy we emit and receive is determined by which of these two energy fields we manifest.

20. I believe each of us has generated (usually unconsciously) a sense of our own competence and worthiness. This self-perception generates an energy field which dominates and importantly directs our life.

21. I believe that by *consciously* investing in the creation of a personally meaningful vision, we can mobilize, purify and direct our energy.

22. I believe this is a crucial act of intentionality; and so the courageous creation of a vision is a profoundly important decision.

Kierkegaard tells us that "Life is not a problem to be solved but a reality to be experienced." Yes! Yes! Yes! What a provocative statement he gives us.

We are standing on a new river, but we don't know it.

Thomas Merton

Chapter IV

SCARCITY, ABUNDANCE
AND BOUNDARY

In mathematics students are introduced to the idea of "prime numbers". A prime number, of course, is a number which is divisible only by itself or by 1. Thus, to the mathematician prime numbers have a certain bedrock, foundational quality. An instructor of mine once referred to prime numbers as "numbers with unquestionable integrity." I regard boundary as the behavioral equivalent of a prime number.

I would like to continue in more breadth and detail my exploration of abundance, another behavioral prime number, and its mirror reversal, scarcity. Quite literally these concepts (and boundary) are the most basic and irreducible elements of personal growth.

Abundance is a constellation of attitudes which, consciously and unconsciously, infiltrate our very being. These attitudes tell us that the *qualities* of life we most dearly prize and greatly cherish are freely available. While we may not yet know how to gather the harvest, this worldview tells us that, as an article of faith, the world is truly bountiful and benevolent … and that this bounty is readily available.

We are able to genuinely rejoice in the prosperity of others. Their success is a validation of our faith. As we witness their abundant joy, we are better able to understand, appreciate and seek for ourselves comparable qualities of life.

What we have learned in developmental psychology tells us that the idea of abundance is at the very core of human existence. *Abundance is natural; it is not something to be learned.* When the early experiences of an infant and child support natural developmental processes, especially during the first five years of life, abundance becomes an outcome. However, when these early experiences distort a child's natural developmental processes, then scarcity becomes a learned mode of compensatory and defensive behavior.

Notice, please, that abundance is not measured by money or things. Because abundance is a quality of life, it cannot be measured. It can only be felt. Thus, abundance is not something we arrive at with our head. Instead we are brought to abundance by the feelings of our heart.

The abundant personality is naturally and easily optimistic. This person has learned that most of the time, good things seem to happen in life. *And when bad things happen, they are the exception.* Because of these experiences, it is easy for the abundant person to see the world as a warm and benevolent place and to find that most of the time, most of the people in the world will be kind. There are exceptions, of course. But these are exceptions, not the rule.

Because of the qualities of life which are enjoyed by an abundant person, feelings of love, warmth and acceptance are spontaneously generated … and received. Fear is an infrequent visitor. And when fear is felt, an abundant person seeks to understand the contextual meaning of fear, for surely fear is not something that is inherent in the individual.

Abundance provides an individual with a sense of inner security. It is an abundant person who can authentically say, "Because I am OK, I will be OK. I don't need to stack the deck. Or wear a belt, suspenders and a parachute. Whatever happens, I will deal with it well. I will learn from the experience and be the better for the experience. And I will be OK."

It is this sense of inner security which permits an abundant person to mostly feel calm, centered and at peace. It is certainly true that abundant people have life crises. Difficult and painful events happen in the lives of abundant people. But abundance provides the individual with a certain resiliency … and perhaps most important, *abundance permits an individual to feel grief, pain or loss, have closure and ultimately move on.*

We must be sure to understand that abundance is *not* the inauthentic "smile regardless of the pain" which many of us have been taught. Nor is abundance a Pollyanna belief that life is the proverbial rose garden. Abundant people are not immune to pain, distress and what the world might regard as failure. But, you see, an abundant person does not subscribe to the nihilistic belief that "shit happens!"

For an abundant person, it is not shit that happens. It is life that happens. And abundance permits an individual to deal with life, realistically and effectively.

By its nature, abundance is transcendent and transformational. I have already pointed out that abundance is a quality of life, and so it cannot be measured. That's the bad news. The good news is that as a quality of life, abundance is not finite. It is infinite. *It is a life force on par with gravity.* The power of this life force cannot be reckoned. But as with love, the more of it you have and the more of it you give, the more of it you receive. The supply is universal and inexhaustible.

We can describe scarcity with less effort. The reason is simple enough; if we hold all of the attributes of abundance in front of a mirror, then scarcity can be readily seen as the mirror reversal of abundance. Let me illustrate by offering you these observations.

Scarcity is not natural. It is the result of distortion of a person's early developmental processes. Scarcity creates a worldview which tells people that they are at risk and vulnerable in an environment that is fundamentally hostile. That's why they are never able to really relax. They must always be on guard and vigilant. Metaphorically they sleep with one eye open. They look at opportunities for joy, fun and fulfillment as illusionary, distracting and unrealistic. Scarce people say those who are happy are somehow being blind to the dangers that are inherent in life. According to scarce people, what appears to be prosperity is a sure sign that someone else has taken an unfair share of the world's bounty… and/or has not played by the rules.

Scarcity tells people that most of their lives must be spent in gathering money and things. If they are "lucky" and good stewards, then in their few remaining years they can pursue (and hope to have) some of the qualities of life which are at the core of the abundant person's every-day experiences.

Scarcity causes a person to become fixated with the measurement of things. And so scarcity leads a person to focus upon acquisition, possession and control rather than enjoyment and the benefit of others. The inevitable consequence of this is that scarcity causes an individual to become primarily invested in *Doing* and *Outcome* rather than *Being* and *Input*.

Since control of outcome is impossible, scarcity contributes to one's sense of inadequacy and, thereby, anxiety. Objects are valued more than experiences. Control is manifested by a need to protect rather than a desire to enjoy or serve.

A worldview of scarcity ultimately constitutes a self-fulfilling prophesy. Barring intervention, scarce people can help themselves to feel better only by circling the wagons even more tightly…and becoming even more scarce. But the sense of security that is derived from becoming more and more scarce is displaced by the fear that someone may yet be able to penetrate those defenses. That's why scarcity *always* involves a pervasive sense of fear, especially the fear of loss, failure, personal inadequacy and/or abandonment. *Fear and love cannot coexist; where there is one, there is the absence of the other.* And so those who have developed a scarce worldview are not able to permit themselves to be participants in truly intimate relationships.

As a person accommodates to a life without intimacy, the compensatory behaviors almost always involve withdrawal, denial and suspicion. And so life becomes preparation for impending gloom, doom and disaster. *Scarce people are inherently pessimistic.* When something good happens to scarce people, it is an exception. And probably it is fate setting them up for a fall. But when something bad happens, it is expected validation of what they already believed: Life is tough; the world is a hostile place; and most of the time, most people will take advantage of you.

The mantra of the scarce person is "Because I'm not OK, I will not be OK. And so I need to do everything I can to stack the deck. Control the variables. Isolate myself. And otherwise prepare for the worst because it will probably happen."

Let me again admire with you Wayne Dyer's distinction: A scarce person counts the number of apples on a tree; while an abundant person contemplates the number of apples in a seed.

Surely we can agree that abundance (and its mirror reversal, scarcity) are crucial concepts in understanding the human condition. Now I would like to join these concepts to my earlier discussion of boundary.

Proposition #1: In the absence of well-developed boundary, it is not possible to develop an abiding sense of abundance. When my boundary is weak, I am gravely limited in the self-esteem which I can generate. A weak boundary permits the precious stuff of my inner reality to flow out and become contaminated. When this happens, my sense of self is limited, even depleted. It is axiomatic that those who have a poorly developed boundary will also lack self-esteem. Should my boundary be weak, I must constantly seek out opportunities to have others affirm my worth. But no matter how hard I try, the good feelings which others give me are soon dissipated. And so I must compulsively work at replenishing the good feelings which I want to receive from others. I do that by learning to please them. *Which means, of course, that I must be more committed to what is outside of me than what is inside of me.*

Proposition #2: Within the human psyche there is an innate spiritual need by all of us to be emotionally connected with others. A sense of community is an aspect of health; and beyond this each of us wants to be part of a web of deeply committed relationships. In Maslow's lovely phrase, we yearn to "belong and be belonged." Community and intimacy require boundary. A well-developed boundary permits a person to have confidence in the intrinsic worth of the inner self. In this circumstance an individual can choose, as an act of health and well-being, to fulfill his/her desire for affiliation, affection and approval.

But when a person's boundary is not well-developed, the inner self is puny. This may generate a driven need for a person to demonstrate s/he does not need anyone. Or in the absence of a well-developed boundary, a puny inner self may strive to sacrificially earn the gratitude of others and, thereby, seemingly gain a sense of affiliation, affection and approval. Both of these strategies are contrary to health and well-being.

Proposition #3: While it is true that all abundant people have well-developed boundaries, it is not true that all people with well-developed boundaries are inevitably abundant. The qualities of life which are associated with abundance cannot exist in the absence of boundary. But the reverse is not true. Abundance is a worldview…a constellation of attitudes. Scarcity, too, is a worldview…a constellation of attitudes. An individual with a well-defined boundary (that is, a keen sense of where self ends and others begin) may have learned to manifest a worldview of scarcity.

Proposition #4: It follows, therefore, that as a person learns to become more abundant, boundary development is a related and synergetic benefit.

Proposition #5: Since abundance is natural and scarcity is a distortion, learning to become more abundant really involves the challenge of unlearning how to be scarce.

Proposition #6: We unlearn something by learning in its place something that is more satisfying.

Proposition #7: The more we learn about scarcity, the more we must acknowledge that all of us have choices. I may be scarce as a consequence of my early life experiences. But as I am able to become more clear about the dynamics of scarcity, I must increasingly take responsibility for my decision to remain scarce.

Proposition #8: This kind of unlearning and learning is experiential. It cannot be acquired from a book (including this book) or any other form of outside/in information processing. Nor can it be learned alone. Experiential learning can only occur in relationship. It involves feelings, not cognition. Ideally, this is the kind of learning which occurs within families...or family surrogates such as a team or within experiential workshop settings. Perhaps the most effective form of experiential learning involves mentoring. Spending time with a person who has qualities of life which you admire and want for yourself is a powerful form of learning.

This simple table may help you to better grasp the flow of my argument:

ABUNDANCE	SCARCITY
Being	Doing
Accepts responsibility for control of input	Strives to attain control of outcome
Qualitative standards	Quantitative standards
Experience-based	Object-based
Intimacy	Isolation
Requires boundary — abundance cannot exist in the absence of a well-developed boundary	Does not require boundary — but scarcity can exist within a well-developed boundary
Transformational	Constrictive
Infinite	Finite
LOVE	FEAR

The vast majority of human beings dislike and even dread all notions with which they are not familiar. Hence it comes about that at their first appearance, innovators have always been derided as fools and madmen.

Aldous Huxley

Chapter V

WHAT IS REALLY REAL?

Sometimes when I work with groups, I'll request that people close their eyes and breathe deeply. I ask them to "see" a beautiful lemon with the eye of their mind. I'll invite them to pick up the lemon…hold it…sniff it…and then scratch it with their thumbnail. Then I ask them to sniff the lemon again. When everyone has opened their eyes, we talk about their response to this simple imaging exercise. Most people comment on how the scent of the imaginary lemon stimulated the flow of their saliva.

Was their saliva stimulated by a real lemon? Was the remembered odor of the rind real? Is it possible for the odor to be real but the lemon to be imaginary? And if the odor is imaginary, then is the flow of saliva real? What does "real" really mean? *Is an object "real" objectively; or is its reality derived from a person's experience of it? Is it the experience which is real…or the perception of the experience?* Is it possible for anything to exist truly independent of one's capacity to experience or perceive it?

These are not new questions. A major area of philosophy (metaphysics) involves the study of these questions; and a vast library has been created by philosophers, theologians, psychologists, mathematicians and social/natural scientists who have responded to these questions.

I want to raise some philosophic questions which may help you to define deeper and more real reality in your own life. *The world is rapidly moving away from the perceived realities which have governed it for the past 350 years; and toward a new perception of what is really real. The observations I'm offering in this section are derived from my understanding of these new perceptions.* Please do not accept my observations as "true"; and I hope you won't reject them as "false". Perhaps my observations can be stepping stones which will lead you to a new, different and important way of seeing the world…and your place in it.

1. In life there are no failures. Only outcomes. Earlier I pointed to one of life's curiosities: We cannot define any quality of life without also referencing its opposite. It's not possible to define "hot" without reference to the idea of "cold". How can we explain "up" except by comparing it to "down"? And "right" makes no sense in the absence of "left". A functional understanding of either "good" or "bad" requires us to possess both ideas, and "on" has no meaning until we grasp the principle of "off". *All qualities of life contain their opposite.* This is an important paradox which seems to be intrinsic to life itself.

Consider "failure" or its apparent opposite, "success". When we do not realize that every quality of life contains its opposite, we tend to regard each of the opposing qualities as entirely separate and unrelated. This permits us to make a moral judgment, consciously or not, about what is "good" and what is "bad".

Some people allege that this situational perspective is counter-scriptural. Yet the ancient Greek word for "sin" is taken from the lexicon of archery, and the word quite literally means "missing the mark". I understand that to mean an unsatisfactory outcome.

The dialogue between Jesus and the woman at the well is a poignant illustration of how this same principle can be applied to an ordinary life situation. It's useful to observe that in the scriptural accounts of this episode, Jesus did not blame or moralize. He did not separate himself from her by defining "good" and "bad" as separate and disconnected states of being. He advised her to stop sinning ... that is, to try to not miss the mark. But he did not judge her. He did not decide that she was "bad".

When an archer's arrow is wide of the mark, the archer has an opportunity to recalculate before shooting the next arrow. The archer can strive to better assess and integrate the variables of wind, draw, bow tension, etc. Then the archer can try again. In speaking to the woman at the well, Jesus was asking her to recalculate the variables of her behavior so that she might choose to try again.

For me it's useful to live in a world where there are no failures. Only outcomes. A satisfactory outcome helps me to more fully become the person whom I hope to be. An unsatisfactory outcome is a barrier to the realization of my self-vision. When I experience an unsatisfactory outcome, I have the choice of learning enough from it so that, in fact, it can be transformed into a satisfactory outcome.

2. It is profoundly difficult to calculate the worth and value of any decision or event. My life and the lives of my family have been touched by a dear friend who talks about outcomes that are "seemingly bad". Within the seemingly bad we may find an ultimate good.

Early on, most of us have received a cultural perspective of life that's similar to what we experienced as a three-year-old while playing with blocks. We learned that life consists of a series of happenings that are mostly rectangular in shape with straight sides and 90 degree angles.

We take these happenings, one by one, and build a foundation. It supports subsequent courses of blocks. If some of our happenings are "bad", then those blocks aren't square and they introduce wobble into our life. Even when we build carefully and with square blocks, should our tower reach too high, it will topple. This cultural metaphor is an important symbol of the scarcity which permeates our society.

When we concern ourselves with the idea of outcome, we begin to see that our experiences are streams and tributaries which flow into the river of our life. Notice that in the prevalent cultural model, each of the child's blocks is separate. A really "bad" experience is like a grossly distorted block; it means that we can't use it to build an admirable life. Notice also that the cultural model is linear ... sequential ... and predictable. Yet what we know (and our experience tells us) is that life is not like this.

While the linear model with square blocks approximates what most of us have learned culturally about life, I am not aware of any scripture or writings in the 10,000 year history of our wisdom literature which describe the processes of life with a comparable geometry. Instead, I note with interest that both the Hebrew and Christian scripture make frequent reference to flowing, non-geometric visual imagery, especially light, water and wind.

3. Any question that can be answered with certainty is not significant. The companion statement is that any question which is significant contains uncertainty and ambiguity. The conclusion is inescapable: When we insist on organizing our lives around certainties (outer reality), we cannot acknowledge the significant issues that are at the very core of living (inner reality).

All the aspects of life which we most dearly prize and greatly cherish are inherently qualitative and, therefore, not measurable, demonstrable, replicable or predictable. Please read this sentence again. Pause over it. Think about it. If you were to agree with it, then what would this sentence mean in terms of how you might choose to manifest the qualities of your life?

For example:

Love. Honor. Integrity. Joy. Fulfillment. Can these be measured? Or demonstrated? Today can I precisely replicate the love that I felt yesterday? Am I able to predict tomorrow's joy? Now this is very practical stuff; there's nothing fanciful about it. Here's why.

When the questions we ask are concrete, specific and measurable, the answers will be, too. Any question which begins with the word, "how", is suspect. "How" questions are not "bad" or "wrong" or "inappropriate". It is as simple as this: When we begin our inquiry by asking "how", we are inclined to not ask "why". But when we begin with "why" questions, we will always ask "how" and most of the time we will be able to develop "how" responses which are direct extensions of our response to the "why" questions. There is a related distinction between "how to" and "why" questions. "How to" is always concerned with outer reality; and "why" questions inevitably challenge us to explore our inner reality. Thus, in a world marked by rapid and discontinuous change, "why" questions always deepen our appreciation of ourselves.

This is no less true in our personal lives than in our businesses. "Why" may be the most powerful word in the language. Why am I here? Why am I affiliated with this business? Why do I expect this business to prosper? Responding to these questions will give us a very different outcome than if we merely ask, "How can this business prosper?"

When I respond to these and similar "why" questions, my words will contain uncertainty and ambiguity. I must courageously continue the process. My responses to each set of "why" questions will stimulate another set of "why" questions. The process is infinitely progressive ... and infinitely valuable. When I am patient with the process, I will be led by my own responses to all of the "how" questions.

In summary: Tactics (outer reality) emanate from strategies, and strategies flow out of values (inner reality).

What is real for me is what I am feeling. What is real for you is what you are feeling. The reality of our relationship is generated by our mutual capacity to give and receive our individual feelings. The process I'm now describing is stimulated when we ask "why" and it is shut off when we ask "how".

4. It follows that any question which can be answered with certainty is not central to our experiences or foundational to our future. It doesn't make sense, therefore, to fret about whether we have the "right" answer. Individually and organizationally, most of us spend countless hours and many ergs of energy worrying about whether we have the "right" answer to a question. If it is an important question, then by its nature a "right" response is not possible and so our effort to be "right" is misplaced.

And if it is a question that can be answered with certainty, we do not need to worry about whether the answer is deemed to be correct. We simply need to act upon whatever response seems appropriate and then see how we feel about the feedback which occurs. *The purpose of decisions is NOT to give us answers. No, no, no! The purpose of decisions is to generate feedback.* Should we open our business an hour earlier or expand the sales force? There is no "right" answer to this "simple" question. But if we decide to alter our practices for a while, we'll establish some new feedback loops...and we will have feelings about those feedback experiences that will tell us whether or not we are being well served by the decision.

5. Uncertainty about outcome ... ambiguity about means ... and confusion about consequences is inherent to all significant change. The reason, of course, is that significant change always involves qualities of life; and these cannot be measured, demonstrated, replicated or predicted. *The issue here involves giving up control.*

When I choose to not tolerate uncertainty, ambiguity and confusion, I am simply saying, "I want to be in control of my outcome." But it is clear that I cannot be in control of my outcome because my outcome is largely determined by a myriad of people and events which are far beyond my reach or influence.

I can only be responsible for me...for acting in ways that are congruent with my feelings. I am responsible for input but not outcome.

This realization is unbelievably freeing. Most of us spend enormous time and energy seeking to control what all of our life experiences tell us cannot be controlled. By letting loose of the attempt, I bring myself great peace and a new abundance of opportunities and energy.

I'm reminded of some words written by Ram Dass in his first book, *Remember Now Be Here*. The book was first published in 1971. Since then more than a million copies have been purchased. The book is something of a latter-day classic.

> The next message is where you are when you hear the next message. Whenever you're ready, you'll hear the next message. The interesting thing is there's always a next message and it's always available…. The funny thing about all the secrets of the East or the secrets of mysticism is that they're not secret! Nobody's saying, "Don't tell them." They're telling you. They're yelling it… In my case I kept reading the books but I didn't understand them. They were yelling the secrets but I couldn't hear them because I was looking at them from the wrong place… I still wanted to know that I knew… I was still Western Rational Man and so I went and I looked and looked and looked, and as long as I looked as a rational man looking, I didn't find anything…

Wow! "I still wanted to know that I knew…. I was still Western Rational Man and so I looked and looked and looked, and as long as I looked as a rational man looking, I didn't find anything…." One of the reasons that Ram Dass is such a treasure is that he started his life as Richard Allen Alpert, Brooklyn, New York, and he earned a PhD in mathematics from MIT. During the late 1950s he earned a PhD in psychology. He then was a visiting professor at the University of California at Berkeley. He was offered a tenured position at Harvard University. While at Harvard, he taught in four different graduate schools and also held research contracts with both Yale and Stanford.

Because he has experienced personally the search of the Western Rational Man, his journey into a different system of logic is especially instructive. As he reminds us, there are logic systems available to us that aren't linear or deductive!

6. All transformations emanate from feelings. Incremental change is stimulated by our intellect. By definition, incremental change involves the intellectual operations of regulation, control and sequential development. But while the presence of regulation, control and sequential development facilitate incremental change, these same functions assure the absence of transformational change. Transformation is an *affective* phenomenon which always draws upon feelings. Feelings cannot be regulated, controlled or kept within a sequential structure.

Feelings are generated by our inner spirit. They are a manifestation of the reality that is within us. Feelings are qualitative; they cannot be measured or compared. Thus, feelings are other than finite. Similarly, a transformation is also an inside/out phenomenon. A transformation cannot be measured or compared. A transformation is other than finite.

7. Significant change cannot be slowly attained. The initial process of clarification can proceed slowly. For example, we can gradually come to acknowledge that we want our future to be different than our past. But clarification ultimately requires trial-and-error. Clarification cannot proceed apart from action. *Without action, clarification is incomplete.* And so at some point we must act;

and until we act, the process of clarification is stalled. *Significant (transformational) change requires fully committed action. We must assume a favorable outcome and act upon the assumption.* We must know that if the outcome is not favorable, the feedback we receive will allow us to make a mid-course correction so that we can again fully commit to a new action. Incremental change allows us to dip a toe in the water. But transformational change requires us to jump into the pool. Here is a corollary to this statement.

8. Our feelings provide the only point of entry for significant, enduring and positive change. To stay with the above example, the initial process of clarification can be cognitive and analytic. But once we have acted, the feedback loop prompts feelings, not cognition. *All enduring and significant change is an extension of affect, not intellect.* There is a second corollary as well.

9. When I commit to significant change, it's not important where I begin. If significant change were solely a function of intellect, the beginning point would be important. That's because cognitive processes *are* orderly. But affective processes cannot be regulated or controlled by an established structure (for example, deductive logic). Feelings are spontaneous and flowing, and so it is not important where I begin. Once I decide to get wet, it doesn't matter where I enter the pool.

10. There are no second-hand experiences. I have the capacity to think about what *has* happened or to contemplate intellectually what *might* happen. But in the here-and-now moment, there are only feelings. My feelings are my feelings. They cannot be explained, defended, justified or rationalized. *Simply because I feel them, my feelings are valid.* Empathy permits me to open myself and receive an approximation of the feelings of others. But no one can *feel* the feelings of another person, and so there are no second-hand experiences.

11. *Process is more important than content.* Because we live in what is culturally perceived as a bottom-line world, these six words create doubt and suspicion in the minds of lots of people. At another time in my life, I was actively involved in a process that is called "focus group interviews". Let me describe a real-life situation. A toy manufacturer wanted to know whether a product's instructions for assembly and use were effective. We brought together several groups of people who approximately simulated those who had historically bought the product. We asked them to assemble and use the product, and then we conversationally explored how they felt about the process.

This is not what my client had initially wanted. The manufacturer had suggested that we observe potential buyers assembling and using the product through a one-way mirror ... that we use a stopwatch to determine how quickly they "got" the message ... and that we tabulate false starts and errors. In a word, the client wanted information about content and information-transfer.

But through the spontaneous interchange of focus group interviews, we were able to tap into this information and a very great deal more. For example: How purchasers felt about the packaging ... the price ... quality of construction ... other available alternatives in the market-place ... and the feelings of purchasers about the performance of the product.

Here is the *true* bottom line: The seemingly objective information which my client originally wanted had no new utility until it was surrounded by the *context* of the user's feelings and impressions.

A while ago I read an essay by a Dutch physician who explored the problem of saying to a parent, "Your child has the measles." This implies, he argued, that measles is an objective entity of known and predictable consequences, and that all children are more or less affected in the same way. He statistically demonstrated the enormous variations in the course of the disease and the idiosyncratic response of apparently similar children. His conclusion: Physicians would be better advised to tell parents that their child was "measling"; the use of this word correctly implies that the child is experiencing a unique event. For him, measles is a process, not an event.

12. An individual's perception of available choice slows the process of significant change. Over the years I have worked with many scores of people who want to sponsor significant change in their lives because intellectually they believe it is in their best interest to do so. This mindset virtually assures their diminished effectiveness. They perceive themselves as having a choice (whether to change); and then they choose to act on an option which they have cognitively selected. *Because they perceive themselves as having a choice, their commitment is less than* complete and, consciously or not, they are, in the best tradition of Western Rational Man, seeking to control their outcome. Notice, also, that in the example I am describing, the process is fundamentally intellectual.

Let me quickly add that this is not in any sense "bad". Indeed, I observe that most people who effectively sponsor significant change in their lives begin similarly. It is by experiencing this process that they come to understand (on the level of feelings) this truth: *The person who is most effective in sponsoring significant change has come to feel that there is no choice. "I must do this. For me there is no choice."* This is the essence of commitment.

Let me cite the lives of two people to illustrate what I mean — Pablo Picasso and Mother Teresa. In so many ways, it would be difficult to find two individuals who are more different. But at least in one crucial regard, their individual lives manifest the same principle. Picasso did not have a choice. He lived his life in the only way that he could live his life. Mother Teresa had no choice. She lived in the only way she could.

For both of them, the choice to have no choice was made on the level of feeling, not intellect. *And because they had no choice, they were able to become truly free.* In their lives, commitment became a pathway to freedom.

13. Those whose personal values are unclear are inclined to see those whose values are exceptionally clear as living in bondage. Thus, many people would interpret the pure commitment of Picasso and Mother Teresa as the absence of freedom. I am reminded of Kris Kristofferson's beautiful lyric, "Freedom's just another word for nothing else to lose." Here we have another paradox: Those whose values are murky have the broadest range of personal choice…but the least freedom. Paradoxically, those with the narrowest range of personal choice have the most freedom.

14. As a person's values become more and more clear, the range of choices narrows until, ultimately, there is no choice. Then one is free! Here is what I mean. Through processes of clarification, each of us has the opportunity to become more and more clear about personal values. For many years, I have abbreviated these processes by asking three simple questions: *Who am I? Who do I want to become? Why?*

In responding to these questions, a person informally creates a statement of basic beliefs which are so intrinsic that if they were to change, the individual would also change. Let me say this in another way: A person's values represent a statement of fundamental beliefs which guide an individual in making choices. As each of us becomes more clear about who we are and who we want to become, we also become more clear about how we must behave if life is to be lived congruently.

One's basic values refer to a series of "I believe…" statements which identify who we are at the core of our being. These "I believe…" statements lead to a series of "I do…" statements that we know as "mission". We come to realize that because I believe "X", I have no choice but to do "Y". As this happens more and more profoundly, my life becomes values-based and mission-driven.

Soon I have no choice, and then I am free.

I am describing this process in terms of an individual. But the process is parallel for any corporate entity or institution. The curious thing here is that a school or church or business enterprise cannot become values-based and mission-driven unless this process is also occurring in the lives of those who are providing leadership.

The reason is simple. As people become more clear about who they are and want to become, they want their values to be mirrored in work. That is the inevitable consequence of personal clarity. Institutional and corporate clarity are an outcome of leaders who are becoming more clear about themselves.

15. No one can "teach" anyone else how to significantly change. It took me a bunch of years to comprehend and appreciate this. But now that I have, it is liberating. Teaching is an act of intellect. Feelings cannot be taught. They can be modeled. They can be facilitated. We can nurture and encourage the realization of affective truths. But we cannot didactically teach them.

16. A focus upon technique often indicates incomplete commitment, still murky values and a retreat from personal relationships. Sometimes those who, consciously or not, are striving to avoid significant change will tend to fixate on the perfection of means (technique). When we talk about techniques, we're usually referencing an instrumental response to a "how" question. Indeed, we use the phrase "how-to" as a semantic alternative to the word "technique". Thus, a concern with techniques is specific, limiting and certainly measurable, demonstrable, replicable and predictable.

Techniques are derived from tactics and tactics emanate from strategies. Strategies flow out of values. When we begin on the outside with techniques, our concern with results inhibits our capacity to move inward and become clear about our values. But when we begin with core values, we must ultimately (and authentically) move outward.

Those who are unclear about core values, or are uncomfortable with them, seem to instinctively develop a fascination with technique as a way of avoiding their pain and confusion. Focusing upon the perfection of technique provides a rational, socially-acceptable reason for *not* beginning to take the risks of meaningful change. Technique becomes an end rather than a means.

17. When we commit to the attainment of a preferred future of choice, it must be with awareness that as we move closer to attainment, we will always be in process of redefining what is preferred. Nowhere is this more dramatically seen than in what used to be called "management by objectives". Whether you have felt the sting of formal instruction in MBO or not, I'm confident that your own life, personally and in your business endeavors, will prove this point:

As we move toward a defined objective, there is always a change in the system. For example, we learn something through our early effort and that may encourage us to move faster or slower ... or to redefine or even abandon the objective ... or perhaps to combine it with other objectives.

Regulations ... pricing ... the competitive situation, etc. are constantly in flux. Our staffing situation is improving ... or maybe it's deteriorating. The variables are endless.

An elegant flow system benefits from all of this input and uses the newly acquired information in a never-ending process of redefinition and redirection. The emphasis is on the process of planning, not The Plan. The situation is dynamic, not static; responsive, not fixed.

In all of our endeavors, most certainly in our personal lives, we can strive to create elegant flow systems which help us to center ourselves in the here-and-now rather than striving to correct the past or assure the future. Planning is a legitimate and crucial function. It is a process without end. The creation of Plans is a sophisticated way of substituting "how" for "why" within a fixed and known timeframe.

18. An anticipation of material reward is more delicious than the reality of possession. But the reality of spiritual reward is more delicious than the contemplation of it. On the most mundane level, compare the intense pleasure of a new automobile with the intense pleasure of helping a child through a difficult growth experience. *When material rewards are not achieved through spiritually satisfying endeavors, then both the person and the rewards become dank. Our ability to materially prosper (not merely succeed, but prosper) is the result of a values-based, mission-driven life.*

19. At a deep level of meaning, we cannot take others where we have not been. Please let me explain by asking you to imagine a series of four concentric circles. The innermost circle at the core of the model represents our "values". The next circle provides context for our "strategies". (Strategy refers to the purposeful ways in which we commit basic resources. Gifts and talents, time, energy, opportunities and money are examples of strategic resources.) Then there is a circle of tactics. And finally an outer circle of how-to "techniques".

The Internal Revenue Service has discovered that some professions have a higher incidence of tax delinquencies and tax cheating than others. For example, CPAs and accountants are on the IRS "hit list" because a disproportionate number of accountants abuse the system.

Here is an example of how a person can have a high level of technical skill with a considerable capacity for directing others...but yet be flawed in his/her own behaviors. At the outer level of technique, it is entirely possible that a person can possess useful information...have considerable skill in communicating it...but live incongruently with what is claimed to be a preferred way of life.

But as we move toward the core of this model, this becomes less and less likely. My ability to help you clarify your values is limited by my ability to have clarified my own. *I cannot take you where I have not been.* At the core of this model, none of us can facilitate in others a level of maturity or integrity which exceeds our own. There is a wonderful Buddhistic fable about a mother who brought her young son to a monk and said, "Tell him not to eat sugar." The monk said, "Please return in two weeks." Two weeks later the mother and son returned, and the monk said to the young man, "Don't eat sugar."

The mother asked, "Why didn't you tell him that two weeks ago?" "Because I was eating sugar," said the monk. Part of our cultural heritage is represented by the axiom, "Do as I say, not as I do." On the level of technique, incongruity is not inevitably an impediment to effective teaching. But on the inner-most level of values and beliefs, integrity and effectiveness require congruence.

20. *Meaningful service to others requires that first we are able to serve ourselves.* None of us can give from empty pockets. It is arrogant for me to believe I can take care of others if I have not yet learned to take care of myself.

21. *When we conceptualize life as a flow model without beginning or end, then each of us is always in process of going to where we have not yet previously been. None of us can ever really return to a place in the past.* This principle, which is basic to General Systems Theory, is sometimes expressed by noting that we can never step twice in the same river. As we put down our second foot, the river has already changed. So it is with our lives. Each experience changes us. We are always in process of becoming. It's useful to think of ourselves as "human becomings" rather than as human beings. But there is an enormous implication embedded in this observation.

If, indeed, I am a human becoming and the river of my life is changing with the passage of every moment, *then who I am is more significant than what I do.* By focusing on who I am rather than what I do, I discover this truth: I am *not* a physician or a banker or a teacher or a brick layer or a parent. I am me, and I have an incredible opportunity to do my work and live my life in ways that both demonstrate and illustrate the unique and constant qualities of my being. When I grasp the power of this opportunity, I am able to realize that in a profoundly meaningful way, there is no physician or banker or teacher or brick layer or parent quite like me. *My life is a celebration of my uniqueness, and my work is a mirror which reflects my uniqueness.*

The more I am able to show people who I am, the more I realize that I am quite literally beyond comparison. I am not a better or worse parent/brick layer/banker/ physician than anyone else. I am me. The personal consequences of this are overwhelming. And in our business endeavors, it means that when I am able to demonstrate my values through my work, then my business is not only beyond comparison … *it is are beyond competition.* Each of us is truly special.

22. When we focus on our probable future, we separate ourselves from the possibility of an optimal future. The difference between "probabilities" and "possibilities" is exquisite and important. Probabilities tell us what we cannot achieve. They are centered upon risks rather than benefits. But possibilities are expansive, liberating and connected to potentialities.

When we calculate probabilities, we are engaging in an analytic process by which a whole is reduced to its molecular components. More becomes less. Possibilities, however, are additive and even synergistic. The process of seeking what is optimal is also integrative. Parts become a whole, and the whole has a meaning and purpose which go beyond the sum of the parts.

23. *That which is practical is not strategic.* There is a place for practicality. But it cannot be in the conceptualization of a strategic process. Strategy means that we are *optimally* reallocating basic resources — *not* according to what is practical, affordable, feasible or attainable. *We cannot conceptualize strategic processes and simultaneously carry with us our prejudices and fears.* We must learn to first "dream the impossible dream"; then we can create measurable processes for the implementation of it. When the order is reversed, we only perpetuate the present.

24. An individual who does not see him/herself as worthy and deserving cannot find redemption in work. And an individual who feels unworthy in his/her work cannot find sustainable happiness or fulfillment in activities that are outside of work. Everything that has been learned about the developmental aspects of self tell us that a person who feels unworthy and undeserving at the core will not be able to compensate in any enduring way through social or vocational attainments. What's in us will inevitably surround us.

Psychologically, philosophically and theologically, my experiences tell me that all of life must be lived inside/out;

and that no amount of measurable success permits an individual to compensate for the self-perception of inner deficiency. Marianne Williamson has written, "Achievement doesn't come from what we do, but from who we are." Her sentence and the insight which it supports is very, very powerful. I believe she has identified a spiritual and psychological truth which must become our life's companion.

25. The greatest risk is in being adverse to risk. A client will sometimes say to me, "I'm risk-adverse." While many people so define themselves, it's unusual to have someone say, "I'm growth-adverse." Yet all growth involves the augmentation of risk because when we grow we are having new (untried) experiences.

Here is exactly the point. The absence of growth is the absence of life...or what we call death. If we are not dead, then we are alive. If we are alive, then we are changing. Frank Conroy asked, "I know I'm not dead. But am I alive?" A poignant question!

The open question is whether we are changing by intent. If we are not, then our change is reactive and we are subjecting ourselves to external forces. But when we choose to change by intent, then we are organizing our lives around people and activities that provide us with fun, fulfillment, opportunities for service and personal effectiveness. The decision to live intentionally is a proactive decision and so it presents the possibility of risk. But the risk of not risking is more risky because it requires us to reactively give up freedom, autonomy and choice.

26. The fear of failure and the fear of success are alternative ways of saying the same thing. They are fused and inseparable. Consider this litany of attributes which are shared by both of these fears: Guilt about the past...anxiety about the future...shame about self...an inability to live with quiet confidence in the moment...the need to control outcome...reluctance to accept the goodness of others and the benevolence of the universe...a prevalence of scarcity...and an absence of abundance.

I love these words by Marianne Williamson from her book, *A Return to Love*:

> Darkness is merely the absence of light, and fear is merely the absence of love. We can't get rid of darkness by hitting it with a baseball bat because there is nothing to hit. If we want to be rid of darkness, we must turn on a light. Similarly, if we want to be rid of fear, we cannot fight it but we must replace it with love. The choice of love is not always easy. The ego puts up terrible resistance to giving up fear-laden responses....

27. Courage does not mean the absence of fear. Courage means the capacity to acknowledge and accept fear ... learn from it ... and walk through it. Consider these words by the same author:

> A spiritual teacher from India once pointed out that there is no such thing as a gray sky. The sky is always blue. Sometimes, however, gray clouds come and cover the blue sky. We then think the sky is gray. It is the same with our minds. We're always perfect. We cannot *not* be perfect. Our fearful patterns, our dysfunctional habits, take hold within our minds and cover our perfection. Temporarily. That is all.

We are still perfect sons and daughters of God. There has never been a storm that hasn't passed. Gray clouds never last forever. But the blue sky does.

Let me join these words with a few sentences that she wrote earlier in this same book. To my ear and heart, the realization she's here describing is magnificently courageous and encouraging.

> I realized many years ago that I must be very powerful if I could mess up everything I touched, everywhere I went, with such amazing consistency. I figure there must be a way to apply the same mental power, then embedded in neurosis, in a more positive way.

28. If someone has done it, it's possible. For more than a score of years, runners sought a four-minute mile. But until Roger Bannister, no one had been able to accomplish this feat. In the six months following Bannister's run, 17 other milers broke the four-minute barrier. *The perception of possibilities rather than probabilities importantly altered the behavioral potential of runners throughout the world.* That's one of the reasons it's so important to have people in our lives whom we admire. Mentors help us to appreciate that if someone has done it, it's possible for us to do it, too.

29. Conflict is, potentially, the raw stuff of creativity. There is no creativity without conflict. Through all of our recorded history, the song of poets and the vision of artists have been seen as divinely derived. Indeed, it can be argued that creativity is a demonstration and an expression of our spirituality. All creation involves newness and so all creation involves conflict. At least, conflict with those who are committed to an old way or perspective.

If psychologically we can realize that conflict is intrinsic to creativity, then conflict itself has a psychological and spiritual purpose. The challenge, therefore, is to master the management of conflict. Not its resolution, suppression or avoidance. From this perspective, placation and compromise of conflict are counter to our spiritual nature.

In learning to manage conflict, we have an opportunity to realize that conflict can be positive, invigorating and unhurtful. Individually and organizationally, the absence of conflict — or its effective suppression and denial — virtually assures stagnation and prohibits creative growth.

Most of us have been raised to believe that our life experiences determine our internal state ... and so conflict has been culturally perceived as unholy. But the reverse is true. *It is our internal emotional/mental state which determines how we experience our lives.* As we are able to learn that conflict is natural, organic and creatively stimulating, we have an opportunity to recast both our human and spiritual potential.

30. *Life is a celebration and each of us is an honored guest.* It may be that these few words comprise the most important statement in this book. Those who aspire to a more complete measure of abundance and prosperity should seek to understand why this statement is so counter-cultural. Mother Teresa said, "There are no great deeds ... just small deeds done with great love." There is a wondrous gift in her wisdom. I believe she is telling us that life *is* a celebration. Each of us *is* an honored guest ... and *all* of us can freely participate.

The celebration is a celebration of life ... and of abundance. Wayne Dyer helps us to understand difference between counting the seeds in an apple (an act of scarcity) and counting the apples in a seed (an act of abundant love).

I am certainly aware of the unspeakable cruelty the inhabitants of this planet inflict upon each other. Yet an Appleseed Society seems more real and more attainable today than yesterday. The horrors are not less. But finally, finally, finally we are coming to realize that these horrors are always and inevitably an expression of scarcity... *and that we have a choice.* It is through the exercise of intent, which means free and knowing choice, that we are able to find abundance. Without choice, there is scarcity. Quite literally we can choose to choose. And by reason of our expectations of abundance or of scarcity, we create the reality which surrounds us.

Fear not. What is not real never was
and never will be. What is real always
was and cannot be destroyed.

Bhagavad Gita

Chapter VI

SEEING WHAT CANNOT BE SEEN

Philosopher Aldous Huxley is the author of an important book, *The Perennial Philosophy*. Written in 1945 and generally deemed to be a classic, many people who are not familiar with the book nonetheless have been touched by its core conclusions.

Huxley had invested many years of serious scholarship in a study of virtually every known religion throughout all of recorded time. Each of these religions had what he referred to as an "exoteric form" characterized by the traditions and rituals of the religion, the revealed literature, the symbology and architecture of places of worship and all the other *material* manifestations of the belief system.

But Huxley also found that each of these religions had an "esoteric core" of beliefs which were codified, explored and explained by a small group of divinely authorized authorities who provided guidance to believers through elaborate and *immaterial* processes of prayer, meditation and ceremony.

Huxley argued that while the range of exoteric expressions is highly diverse, *the esoteric core of this vast array of religions has an extraordinary similarity*. More precisely — throughout recorded history all religious expressions appear to draw upon a set of universal spiritual truths and experiences. Huxley referred to these shared truths and experiences as "the perennial philosophy". In my writings, I've preferred to identify this common core of spiritual truths as the "wisdom literature"; our terminology differs, but our meanings are the same.

The great French poet, Saint-Exupery said, "Truth is not that which is demonstrable. Truth is that which is ineluctable." The last word in this quotation literally means "that which cannot be escaped or avoided". Classic science deals with what can be demonstrated. But the perennial wisdom, which is shared by all religions throughout all of time, insists that the ineluctable (or that which cannot be escaped or avoided) can only be found through an exploration of (and an identification with) the deep self.

There are many interesting aspects to Huxley's conclusion. For example, consider "truth" as Charles Darwin came to know it. Darwin was surely a man of extraordinary brilliance, and his findings are central to our perception of the world. Today virtually every person has at least a vague idea of Darwin's theories for they have become part of our cultural heritage as well as foundational to scientific knowledge. But few of us remember a French biologist who lived during the same period — Jean Baptiste Chevalier de Lamarck — whose theories were displaced by Darwin's conclusions. Lamarck's stubborn defense of his own theories caused him great personal pain and public ridicule.

Darwin helped us to understand the genetic process of inheritance and the dynamic principles which explain biological diversity. *Lamarck insisted there was also an inheritance of learned information: Acquired knowledge was transmitted inter-generationally without the reoccurrence of formal learning.*

Lamarck's reputation as a thinker and a scientist is in process of rapid rehabilitation. Part of the reason relates to the well-documented work of a Harvard psychologist, Dr. William McDougall, a little-remembered investigator whose impeccably maintained data (assembled nearly a half century ago) are today being rediscovered and honored.

McDougall sought to determine whether there was a scientific demonstrable basis for Lamarck's central thesis that learned patterns of behavior are inherited. He placed rats in a cleverly designed water tank from which they could escape only by swimming to an unilluminated gangway. However, the rats had a choice. They could also swim to a brightly lighted gangway. But this choice caused a rat to receive an electric shock. McDougall carefully recorded the number of errors made by his rats before they learned to swim directly to the unlighted gangway. He continued his experiments for more than 15 years and during this period he tested 32 generations of his rat population. *His data indicate that from the first to the last generation of rats, there was more than a ten-fold increase in the rate of learning.*

Perhaps more surprising, when separate studies in Scotland and Australia were designed to replicate McDougall's experiments, the first generation of rats in both countries learned almost as rapidly as McDougall's 32nd generation. In both Scotland and Australia, a number of rats even "learned" the task immediately without making a single error. Members of the same specie, though physically separated from the rats which had experientially gained knowledge about how to escape, were able to beneficially utilize the knowledge despite their physical separation.

The astonishing work of Dr. Rupert Sheldrake was first described in his book, *A New Science of Life*, published in 1981. Sheldrake, whose scientific credentials are impeccable, is persuaded that all of us are influenced by "morphogenic fields" which represent a cumulative record of past behaviors. Those behaviors especially effective for a specie, according to Sheldrake, are favorably weighted in the morphogenic field. Sheldrake finds evidence that these successful behaviors are inheritable — a form of "natural selection" which goes far beyond Darwin and which cannot be explained by the presence or alteration of either genes or DNA.

Sheldrake rediscovered McDougall's work and replicated his findings in a somewhat different way. Sheldrake constructed a complex maze and was able to demonstrate that over a period of time the ability of rats to solve the maze was increased in successive generations. Sheldrake also confirmed McDougall's finding that in ways which cannot yet be explained, inherited knowledge was somehow made available to members of the same specie, even when they were separated by thousand of miles.

Sheldrake has been responsible for finding situations in nature which cannot be readily explained except by postulating the presence of morphogenic fields and what Sheldrake calls "formative causation". Perhaps the best known of Sheldrake's natural examples is the European cuckoo bird which lays its eggs in the nest of birds of other species. The young, hatched and reared by unwitting foster parents, never see their biological parents. Toward the end of the summer, adult cuckoos migrate to their winter home in southern Africa. A month or so later, the young cuckoos congregate and migrate to the same region of Africa where they join their elders.

Somehow they instinctively know that they should migrate and they know when to migrate. They instinctively recognize other young cuckoos and together they generate a social organization. Finally, they instinctively know in which direction they should fly and they instinctively know when they have arrived. Willis Harman, in his important book, *Global Mind Change*, asked whether the young cuckoos are somehow able to tune into the Great Cuckoo Mind in the Sky and take their directions from there.

Perhaps Harman's words are frivolous. But the idea he raises is profound beyond words. The more we learn about these matters, the more plausible it is that Carl Jung's concept of a collective unconscious goes beyond the mystical and has a credible scientific basis.

Bell's Theorem, a foundationstone of contemporary quantum physics, states that when two subatomic particles have been associated within an atom and then are separated in space, they are "connected" nonetheless. When one of them is perturbed in certain ways, the other one is identically affected — and instantaneously. *The connectedness between them apparently does not depend on some kind of "signal"; the event occurs even when the particle is separated from the atom by thousands of miles. An event takes place for which there is no cause. In a scientific culture which is founded upon the principle of causality, this is more than a little disturbing.* Scientifically we are now able to say that everything is connected to (and is influenced by) everything. Nothing and no one is truly alone. Moreover — apparently what has been known in the past can be known again, if only we prepare ourselves to receive the information. And everything we learn that is apparently new has cosmic existence which goes infinitely beyond us.

o o o

Let me now turn a corner and share some early personal history. Once upon a time, in another life, I was a management consultant primarily working with large corporations. Through a series of "coincidences", the excellence of my work gave me an opportunity to specialize in the management of disasters. I waited patiently for a coal mine to explode or a plane to fall from the sky or for someone to insert rat poison in a grocery store product or for a corporate officer to accept a bribe or steal millions of dollars.

The work was frantic and I had a love/hate relationship with what was required of me. Often I would work 16 or more hours a day, seven days a week, for endless weeks ... or even months. While I complained bitterly about the expectations that were placed upon me, I loved the fees that I was able to earn and I was exhilarated by being the commander under battlefield conditions. Most of all, I relished the praise I received from my clients.

At this point in my life, I was not at all contemplative and I was almost totally devoid of insight. I was hooked by excitement and rewards. *By allowing myself to physically and emotionally abuse me, I was able to justify my abuse of others.* Today I understand that as a child there was an enormous amount of chaos in my life; and that the coincidences which led me to this work were not coincidences at all. They were an unconscious attempt to re-create the chaos of my childhood — only this time I would give myself an opportunity to deal with the chaos in a more productive way. As a child, I was a victim. But at this stage of my adulthood I was able to victimize others by the abusive demands that I placed upon them.

As I created and directed my own redemptive psycho-drama, I caused great pain and hardship for people whom I dearly loved. But at the time, I didn't understand this except that it made me angry that the people who I was hurting did not appreciate what I was doing for them.

Unlike my clients, family members did not acknowledge my sacrifices with gratitude. An awareness that what I was doing I chose to do, and the realization that I alone was the true beneficiary of my dysfunctional behaviors, not my clients or family members, called for a level of maturity which at that time of my life was far beyond my reach or even my imagination.

I slowly came to recognize my addictive behaviors . . . and even more slowly I learned to separate from them. Gradually, very, very gradually I began to understand that on the molecular level of being, I had intrinsic worth and value . . . that I could be loved and accepted for who I am rather than what I do . . . and so, therefore, my value was not predicated upon my accomplishments but, instead, my value was a function of my character, integrity, honor and knowledge. In summary — my Being.

For the first time I was able to offer myself a choice which, as you know from my earlier discussion, I now regularly raise for the consideration of my clients:

I AM WHAT I DO VERSUS I DO WHAT I AM.

Along the way I started to realize that when I could confidently accept my value as a Being, my Doing was more creative and effective. It is a useful oversimplification for me to understand that my life's journey has involved moving from the first condition to the second condition.

True learning is not a linear process. In order to give up my frantic, driven behaviors, I had to also accept that my value as a Being was not determined by my Doing. But I couldn't learn this as an abstract truth. I had to learn it experientially. And so I was constantly striving to resolve the paradox of how I could become before I was.

Over the past 20 years, I've work consultatively with scores of men and women who, for reasons peculiar to their individual histories, were workaholics. They had become snared in an obsessive-compulsive trap of their own making. My own life experiences — and the experiences I've had with my clients — have persuaded me that the resolution of this fear-based addiction is an inside/out journey. I can support and facilitate the internal processes of another person. I can raise questions which from time to time my clients would find meaningful. I am able to applaud their gains and join with them in mourning their losses. But ultimately I must acknowledge (and my clients must comprehend) that this journey requires each of us to find and walk our own path. It is a solitary journey.

I've also learned that fear and scarcity are Siamese twins whose presence inevitably point towards serious (but often occult) issues of self-esteem and primal worthiness. And that love (beginning with love of self) displaces fear and scarcity.

○ ○ ○

As adults we live most of our lives with our brain in a problem-solving mode that produces the characteristic brain wave we know as Beta. From time to time we are able to slow our neurological activity as evidenced by a characteristically different brain wave pattern we know as Alpha. *Those activities which are time-less best generate Alpha.* For example — staring into a fire or losing ourselves in the rhythm of the surf pounding on the beach. Allowing a favorite concerto to wrap itself around us. Looking deeply into a favorite painting or becoming a soul without a body as we are lyrically transported by a poem. Prayer and meditation are time-less activities which generate Alpha. So also does biofeedback. The activity is irrelevant; what's important is attainment of time-less tranquility ... a quality of deep inner peace and well-being.

During Alpha we permit ourselves to experience this quality of tranquility and peacefulness. As we move beyond the constraints of time, we leave sequence, order, logic, analysis and, in general, all other modes of problem-solving behind us. By permitting this to happen, we gain access to our creativity ... our imagination and, indeed, to our soul. And so it is here in Alpha that we find our way. *It's another one of those damned paradoxes.* By not seeking to solve a problem, we prepare ourselves to ultimately discover a superior solution; *and we open ourselves to receiving what a friend of mine calls "natural knowledge" — knowledge that we know or can access but which we have not in any formal sense learned.*

Of course, this violates our industrial mentality and our puritan heritage. If there is a problem to be solved, then we must solve it by dint of hard and focused effort. Culturally we have learned that we don't solve problems by meditating or walking on the beach or listening to music or reading a poem. These are all distracting leisurely activities which we can allow ourselves to enjoy for limited periods of time. They are privileges which we earn by reason of our skill in problem-solving. Culturally we begin to learn this at a very young age and as adults it has become an assumed and unexamined mental model. *Worse than that, culturally it is irresponsible to question this mental model.* To doubt the model's legitimacy is diversionary and distracting and irrelevant. It's the choice of lazy people or ignorant people or people who are willing to accept a life of modest attainment.

The more we are able to utilize our Alpha energy, the greater is our effectiveness. I'd like you to consider the possibility that the culturally sanctioned mental model is incredibly counterproductive. The industrial mode of problem-solving may solve problems. But only superficially and repetitively *and always at cost of our creativity, genuine productivity and happiness*. We cannot think our way to great solutions. This was understood by Andrew Carneige, an industrial icon; but it was not understood by Lee Iococca who too was an industrial icon.

Because we cannot think our way to great solutions, I cannot ask you to cognitively arrive at a decision to deliberately seek ways of Alpha enrichment. This is an inside/out process that must be experienced. Each of the experiences is small. But the cumulative value of the experiences is overwhelming. A close study of those men and women who throughout the millennia have accomplished great things will demonstrate that their achievements generally move beyond logic and into the realm of meta-logic that I am here referring to as Alpha. Let me say this another way.

The spiritual truths which surround us are infinitely more powerful than the force of our logic. These spiritual truths have been gathering for ten thousand years. They have a cosmic significance which defies cognitive belief. All the world's religions and all the great religious leaders may argue cognitively over dogma and doctrine. But they share an appreciation for the wisdom literature.

You have access to this empowering body of spiritual truths. There are two ways. Like Huxley, you can devote your life to the study of the world's religions and the great men and women of saintly devotion. Or you can develop your own ways of activating the Alpha energy that is inherently within you, a spiritual gift that separates you from all other forms of life.

With Alpha, you prepare yourself to gather and apply the accumulated wisdom of those who have come before you. It sounds too simple. In fact — it is simple. But learning to open yourself to receive "natural knowledge" is a slow process which requires a robust and mature sense of self.

Natural knowledge is accessed by the attitudes we generate. *Our inner reality has the power to alter our outer reality.* I remember when my daughter Martha was six years old and enjoying a gymnastics class. Her instructor had the kids learning some maneuvers on a balance beam that was set flat on the gym mat. The girls became quite proficient. A few weeks later the beam was raised just a few inches above the floor. That slight difference made a huge attitudinal difference which, in turn, severely restricted the kids' ability to perform what in earlier weeks came easily to them. Perhaps this simple story has some application in your life. Certainly the anecdote illustrates the formative power of attitude on one's inner reality.

There is a third choice, of course. You can continue to depend upon your intellect to set you free. *I've been there and done that, and I know it is not the way.* I also know that the greatest thinkers of the world have learned that their power is not in their thinking. They have learned to move beyond pure cognition to a mystical meta-logic. My observation is they learned to go beyond pure cognition by immersing themselves in the wisdom literature.

Here are some questions you may want to ask yourself:

1. Is my life today marked by the quality of fulfillment to which I aspire?

2. Deep in my heart, do I believe that my accomplishments are properly in scale with my potential?

3. Is my life now largely governed by conscious and unconscious calculations of probability?

4. Do feelings of fear and scarcity permeate my being, even during the moments when I am experiencing success?

5. Do I construe my life as a footrace against time, and I am somehow increasingly persuaded that the faster I run, the more clear it is that I'm losing the race?

6. Are the qualities of life which I most admire least available to me?

7. Do I ask myself to pay a high price for brief interludes of time-less happiness?

Ask yourself these questions with purity of intent, and permit yourself to answer them — quietly and silently and with heroic courage. Some who read these words, in the solitude of their soul, will not be pleased by their responses. If that is true of you, then let me suggest that you have a choice ... the choice is entirely yours ... you do not need the approval or permission of any other person to activate your capacity for choice. And, perhaps most important, the decision to *not* choose is itself a choice.

Life lies always at some frontier, making sorties into the unknown. Its path always leads further into truth. We cannot call it trackless because as the path appears, it seems to have always been there awaiting one's steps. Thus the surprises. Thus the continuity.

M. C. Richards

Chapter VII

MARSHMALLOW ASPECTS
OF BOUNDARY DEVELOPMENT

The year was 1968. It was a beautiful Labor Day weekend. I was napping on my living room couch when the force of an explosion threw me some four feet and I awakened in fright on the floor. The Navy Blue Angels were providing an air show for the city. Two jets collided in mid-air. One of them missed the peak of my roof by some 30 feet. The plane crashed in the street and threw its burning fuel forward — away from my home. Had the same angle of declination been pointing toward my home, I would have been killed. Several houses were demolished. Lives were lost. I was sure my family was outside. Perhaps visiting friends across the street. It was a scary time.

Almost immediately there were many thousands of people clogging the area. Everyone wanted to be at point zero of the disaster. Fire engines, police cars and ambulances were striving to reach the crashed airplane by driving on lawns; there was no way to clear the streets. Emergency vehicles seemed to move forward a few inches at a time in an insane jerk-and-stop process.

The pilot's grotesquely bent dead body was suspended from a tree in my yard. I could not believe what I was witnessing. Scores of people were fighting for the privilege of climbing my tree to reach the pilot. Not to provide help but to remove a boot or cut a piece of his flying suit as a bizarre memento. I still have a clear recollection of the face of a man who broke my kitchen window with a rock so he could take a glass from my counter and draw some drinking water from my sink. Television reporters freely opened the front and rear doors to my home … entered without explanation or invitation … and used my electricity to operate their equipment.

It was a Kafka-like story in which an unbelievable event caused "normal" people to become unbelievably mad, threatening and cruel. Under ordinary circumstances, these normal people likely would have had sufficient boundary and impulse control to function within a cultural norm. But as they endured extraordinary stress, their boundary development was not sufficient to keep them from reverting to immature (even primal) behaviors which, of course, are marked by a loss of impulse control and a dulling of empathy. If the people climbing my tree had been able to see themselves on film as I was seeing them in real time, they would have been shocked into disbelief.

There are at least two widely known studies in the literature which suggest that there may be a similar capacity for madness in all of us. Some years ago, psychologists had a replica of a prison built in the basement of a building on the campus of Stanford University. Through advertisements in the student newspaper, undergraduates were invited to apply for a summer opportunity that would pay them well for two weeks of their time. Each applicant was carefully tested and interviewed by three highly qualified clinicians. Their purpose was to select the 30 students who presented with the highest level of emotional maturity.

These mature students were randomly divided into two groups — 15 "prisoners" and 15 "jailers". The jailers were given the responsibility of responding to the prisoners' needs. Food. Water. Exercise. Recreational opportunities. Etc. The jailers had the authority to create a program for their prisoners and to implement it. *After several days, the supervising psychologists aborted the experiment because these emotionally healthy jailers were jeopardizing the mental and physical well-being of their prisoners.* (As an aside, if this happened with emotionally mature participants in a surrogate prison on the campus of an esteemed university, consider for a moment what almost certainly is taking place in the jails and prisons which you support with your tax dollars.)

A similar (and justly famous) experiment was designed and conducted by a Yale University psychologist, Dr. Stanley Milgram. His findings are especially valuable because he was able to complete the experiment. Dr. Milgram recruited people to participate in what they were told was a study of the impact of punishment on learning. Students were recruited to function as "teachers"; Dr. Milgram then strapped a "learner" into a chair, connected an apparatus to the learner and told the teacher to orally test the learner. Each time the learner gave an incorrect response, the teacher was told to administer an electric shock. With each error the intensity of the shock was increased from 15 volts ("slight shock") to 450 volts ("danger — severe shock").

The teacher did not know that the learners were theater arts majors at Yale or professional actors, and that the apparatus delivered no shock at all regardless of the dial setting. The learners were instructed to wince a little with low level shocks … then grunt and cry… and finally plead with their teacher. (*"Please stop. Get me out of here. I can't stand the pain."*) Several learners were so accomplished in their acting ability that they cried real tears. Some of the teachers were oblivious to the discomfort of the learners. And those who seemed to hesitate or who showed concern were encouraged by the supervising psychologist to continue the experiment. Nearly two-thirds of the teachers punished their learners all the way to 450 volts.

When these learners were interviewed after the experiment about why they did not stop, there was a common theme in each of their responses: *"I was paid for doing this. I had to follow orders. I was told to go on. The supervisor did not ask me to stop."* One teacher, a 43-year-old water inspector said, *"I figured Yale University knows what's going on, and if they think it's all right, well, who am I to think differently?"*

The experiment at Yale apparently supports the common defense of the Nazis who were tried for war crimes. *"It wasn't me who decided to do this. I was simply following the orders of a superior officer."*

What does the behavior at my home or Stanford University's prison or the Milgram experiment tell us about the human condition? This is a profoundly important question which cannot be quickly or easily answered. Surely the boundary development of these young men and women is a factor. A great deal is known about the phenomenon of "dependency" and how dependency intrudes on the development of personal initiative and, ultimately, on the integrity of an adult. There is also considerable clinical information about the relationship of boundary development to emotional dependency.

And so I ask: Is it possible that to some degree, our adult behavior under stress was pre-conditioned by early social/cultural experiences we had as children?

In Daniel Goleman's book, *Emotional Intelligence*, he reports on a well-known experiment involving four-year-old children and marshmallows. The design of the experiment is simple. After establishing a relationship with a four-year-old child, a psychologist produces two marshmallows. The child is told to make a choice: One marshmallow now or two marshmallows "in a little while". Those who chose deferred gratification went to a play room for 15 minutes, and then received their double reward.

Both sets of children (one-marshmallow kids and two-marshmallow kids) were evaluated longitudinally through adolescence. A clear trend was documented: *The two-marshmallow children were consistently more confident, more competent, more assertive, more reliable and, in the face of difficulties, less likely to quit.*

Those children who had experienced the world as a warm and trusting place brought to this experiment a sense of themselves which permitted the choice of deferred reward.

Without a well-developed boundary, a child would not have been able to make this choice. One-marshmallow kids are not bad or dumb. They are simply kids whose early life experiences have already taught them the wisdom of a bird-in-hand. Barring significant intervention, the lessons learned by both one-marshmallow kids and two-marshmallow kids will be carried into their adult life.

Two-marshmallow kids are also preparing themselves for "future-focusing", a term introduced by Dr. Ben Singer when he was a sociologist at Harvard University. Future-focusing by an adult is a powerful extension of a child's capacity to accept deferred gratification.

I became aware of Singer's work through the late, great Robert F. Barkley who aptly applied both the term and the concept to his profession of dentistry. Singer, who himself was raised in a south Boston slum, wondered what had allowed him to become a professor at Harvard while so many of his friends were still slum-dwellers, addicts, prisoners or had died a violent death.

He was able to demonstrate that children who had the capacity to vividly imagine themselves behaving differently in a future time frame had a markedly increased probability of being able to leave the slum. In comparison, those who could not imagine themselves as living a better life outside of the slum would almost certainly perpetuate their living conditions.

There are three aspects to future-focusing: A vividly specific vision; a constellation of new behaviors; and a future time frame. *In my consultative work, I have come to understand that until my client can vividly see him/herself living by intent in a future time-frame, there is little possibility of true transformation.* "You gotta believe!" brought the New York Mets to a pennant. Their rallying cry is based on a sound and important principle of behavior. This is a more casual way of repeating what William James has told us: Our inner attitudes can, in fact, alter our outer reality.

In her book, *Imperfect Control: Our Lifelong Struggles With Power and Surrender,* Judith Viorst tells us that "Self control has two meanings: Constraint (the delay of gratification) and Mastery (the gratification that comes from feeling effective and in charge)."

There is considerable data in support of the proposition that a child's capacity for constraint and mastery begins very early in life. Probably before the eighth week. I like the way Ms. Viorst has summarized this experiment:

> In an experiment with three groups of eight-week-olds, each infant was provided with a special air pillow that responded to the pressure of its head by closing a switch. In one group — let's call it Group A — a mobile of colored balls, hanging over each infant's crib, spun for a few seconds whenever the pillow was pressed by the infant's head. In Group B the mobile also spun, but its spinning did not depend on the infant's actions. Group C, given a stabile, not a mobile, were not able to experience either movement or control.

The infants of Group A, having learned that they could control the movements of the mobile, demonstrated their knowledge by greatly increasing the number of times they pressed the pillow. The others did not. Three or four days into the experiment, Group A infants spent significantly more time smiling and cooing.

Controlling our surroundings clearly brings pleasure. And so with increasing purposefulness and awesome determination, we strive through our first year of life to expand our mastery and to broaden our control.

Common sense tells us that the four-year-olds who were able to defer their gratification and receive two marsh-mallows probably had a qualitatively different infancy and young childhood than those who did not. Remember, please, that the abilities of the two-marshmallow kids to control their personal environments in socially positive ways extended well into adolescence and became the basis of important life skills. The study is on-going and I am confident that the two-marshmallow kids will as a group have quality of life benefits at age 43 or 67.

My own life experiences — and what I have observed in others — surely suggests that confidence, competence, assertiveness, reliability and the ability to productively persevere are characteristics which, when present in adolescence, will likely be carried forward into adulthood. Conversely, when a young child moves through adolescence without having learned the lessons of constraint and mastery, the adult will carry forward these deficits, and they will tend to cause an erosion of the adult's personal effectiveness.

Perhaps some of us who are now age 43 or 67 may suspect that as eight-week-old infants we did not have an opportunity to begin to experience constraint and mastery. Perhaps we might also wonder whether at age four we would have been a one-marshmallow child. (*"Don't take chances. Be careful. Don't be greedy. Don't be selfish. Something is better than nothing. A bird in hand. . . . Half a loaf is better than none. Etc."*) I received these messages, and I suspect that many of you did, too.

When as an adult we courageously examine our own confidence, competence, assertiveness, reliability and perseverance, we may see in ourselves qualities which tend to nullify these aspects of personal empowerment. We may even recognize that our fear and skepticism does not permit vivid future focusing.

In this circumstance most of us have learned a wide range of sophisticated coping strategies. For example — I have known adults who, based on appearance, economic attainments, title and other outer-reality standards, seem to warrant our admiration and emulation. Yet sometimes these apparently successful people persistently (perhaps subtly) rely on patterns of self-sabotage. Often they have difficult personal relationships and may chronically suffer the pain and anguish of depression and anxiety.

The presence of apparently effective coping strategies are not evidence of sickness, a character flaw or a moral failing. And, of course, these coping strategies are learned behavior, entirely separate from our individual packet of DNA.

These (and other) coping strategies are signs of strength, not weakness. They were created by a child as a means of assuring satisfactory passage from today to tomorrow. The revelation that as adults, we can lay aside these inauthentic tactics is powerful beyond words.

Dependency is the word we use to identify an individual who, for whatever reason, cannot claim and develop latent personal power; and so a psychological contract is negotiated with another person whose ego needs are served by accepting responsibility for the dependent person's outcomes. One frequent sign of dependency is reactivity, an often unconscious desire to *not* be seen as a significant person. Paradoxically, fear and an obsessive need to be right are often related to dependency.

The strategic question remains: *"If I were today the person who I hope to become, how would I respond to this situation?"* As we learn to feel the feelings that are generated by this question and respond in a way that honors those feelings, we move ourselves beyond tactics and toward personal empowerment.

A great deal of intelligence can be invested in ignorance when the need for illusion is deep.

Saul Bellow

Chapter VIII

TODAY — AN HISTORICAL PIVOT

H. L. Mencken wrote: "There is no problem not open to a simple, direct and erroneous solution." The hypothesis of this discussion is simple; the proof is not. Here is my hypothesis:

> Since about 1950, the Western world has been experiencing profound and basic change. The rate of change is extremely rapid, and it is accelerating. The quality of change is profound, discontinuous and unpredictable. *While it is tempting to attribute these changes to passing fad or fashion, in fact they relate to the essential conceptual core of how our culture perceives itself, its members and its institutions.* While all of the Western world is affected (and, therefore, all of the non-Western world as well), those nations which are the most advanced by Western (*i.e.*, industrialized) standards are also the most affected.

Should this hypothesis be correct, in 50 years it will be clear that what we are now enduring is an historical pivot point. *We are in the process of becoming something different than we are or were.* Change which is this fundamental and evocative does not often happen. If we begin some 400 years prior to the birth of Christ, at the time of the flowering of ancient Greece, most scholars would agree that there have been only a dozen or so of these historical pivots. Not surprisingly, the frequency of occurrence has increased with the passage of time.

Some of you may take exception to an item or two on the listing which follows. Please do. Others may want to combine two or more entries. Please do. A few may be prompted to add new material to the list. Again, please do. I do not argue that this list is infallible or complete. But I believe that on a conceptual level, the weight and movement of what we are here observing provides a valid basis for anticipating tomorrow.

I do not endorse, approve or argue against any of these particulars. Why argue that grass would be better if it was purple? The reality of my world includes green grass and, as well, the observations which follow are also part of my world. These observations are offered descriptively, not judgmentally. You, of course, are entitled to construct reality as you perceive it in your world. Please understand that while I am using 1950 as the beginning of the pivot period, your birthdate is irrelevant. *Your attitudes are not.* Thus, some of you born after 1950 will feel pre-1950 attitudes toward part of these entries. And the reverse.

Enough of this introduction. Let me begin by acknowledging that each of these points warrant a detailed discussion. That is not now feasible. So I have chosen to think of these briefly described entries as separate pieces which, if you wish, you can arrange in a mosaic that is meaningful to you. But, of course, these pieces are not separate. They are dynamically inter-connected.

1. Prior to 1950, our cultural attitudes told us that revolutions (political revolutions, revolutions of ideas and technology) were responsible for producing radical change. Today we are becoming aware that radical change brings revolutions. Prior to 1950, change was the effect; revolution was the cause. Now we are sensing that change is the cause and revolution is the effect.

2. Before 1950 (indeed, since the early 1600s) our culture has been data-based and deductive. Deduction is the mode of thinking which became our cultural model with the advent of the scientific method. The scientific method establishes an hypothesis which is an extension of a series of "facts". Facts are, by definition, historical. Now, however, radical change tends to be the result of inductive reasoning. By definition, induction proceeds forward from first principles, not from historical (factual) knowledge. The first controlled nuclear fission had no data base; indeed, it violated all known (historical) facts. So does acupuncture. What we know about the autonomic nervous system does not factually permit biofeedback. Our real (factual) knowledge of physics cannot comprehend extrasensory and parapsychological phenomena. The reality of a parapsychic energy source in all of us, during life and after death, has been demonstrated though not explained. The aura of Kirlian energy has no factual explanation.

These are a few examples of how radical change is being derived through an inductive process which is not dependent upon an historical data base. In each of these examples, ideological revolutions are the result of radical change rather than the cause of them. Let me summarize: The inductive method prompts vision before there is understanding; and understanding prior to technology.

3. Prior to 1950, it was generally believed that changing an individual's behavior requires a high level of motivation by the person who is changing and/or a therapeutic relationship. Since 1950, we have begun to understand that individuals do not have to change for behavior to change. We now know (and are beginning to understand) that by changing organizational structure (the formal and informal ways by which a group functions) and organizational climate (the attitudes which group members have toward structure), we are able to significantly alter an individual's behavior within a group without therapeutic intervention.

4. Prior to 1950, learning was regarded as a formal activity involving a pupil who, by definition, knew less than an authority with the assigned responsibility for teaching him. Since 1950, self-discovered learning has been self-discovered; and there is a heightened awareness of the value of experiential (rather than didactic) learning. Since all institutions have a proclivity to maintain the past, this self-discovery has been by learners, not teachers.

Thus, learners have learned that through the sharing of experience, they can bring about participatory learning experiences which are not based upon an authoritarian model. These participatory learning experiences are enormously powerful and, therefore, profoundly effective.

Post-1950 attitudes are quite open to inductively derived phenomenological input — biofeedback, ESP, parapsychology, acupuncture, Kirlian aura, etc. The reason is straightforward: Post-1950 people tend to be open to and accepting of feelings while the actions of pre-1950 people are derivative of facts.

5. Post-1950 attitudes are importantly centered on identity of self. The individual strives for personal fulfillment, an active sense of self-determination (by which a person acts rather than reacts) and a lyrical feeling that joy is a natural condition of humankind.

(It is my personal belief that the resurgence of interest by young people in spiritual expression is linked to these attitudes.) In this environment, the traditional concept of human rights is becoming less centered in property rights, and related material rights, and more centered in opportunities for the individual to strive for self-actualization — which can include material possession but is not its equivalence.

6. For all of these reasons, there is a growing tendency for the attitudes of post-1950 people to incorporate the belief that health, physical and emotional, is humankind's natural state: That ecological and environmental conditions are a primary determinant of health; that active intervention by an ordained authority in a disease process is less necessary than earlier generations supposed; and that, increasingly, health is a multi-factorial personal expression of well-being which is established and maintained by an individual, not institutionally delegated.

7. Because post-1950 attitudes are basically derived from an inductive process, direct, personal here-and-now experience is esteemed while historical and surrogate descriptions of experience are questioned.

8. That is why the pre-1950 personality tends to evaluate a situation in which there is personal risk by asking, "How can I minimize any possible loss?" The essence of this question, psychologically and philosophically, produces a mindset that is not compatible with the post-1950 personality who, when confronting personal risk, is inclined to ask, "How can I maximize possible gain?" Both of these questions are contextual and symbolic of their respective eras. They do not stand alone.

9. There are no rules about leaping into the unknown; no one has yet been there to establish rules. For the same reason, there is an inherent contradiction in the phrase, "future facts". If something is a fact, it exists in the present or the past. When it is encompassed by a future time frame, it is not a fact because all facts are deductive. The behavior of pre-1950 personalities is influenced by time past and time present while post-1950 people tend to use time future as their gyroscope. "Today I am shaping my future" is a post-1950 attitude.

10. Post-1950 personalities tend to find the purpose of organizations and institutions outside their formal structure while their pre-1950 counterparts generally finds organizational purpose within the formal structure of the group. The post-1950 personality strives to develop organizational relationships which encourage inductive conceptual searching that is task-oriented, not time-contained.

11. A related and significant phenomenon is the inclination by the pre-1950 personality to link responsibility to education. But the post-1950 mentality tends to break that linkage. For example, 19 and 20 year-old pilots in the Israeli air force fly technologically advanced jet fighters secured from the USA, France and Belgium. Yet in the USA, pilots of the same aircraft are required to hold a bachelor of science degree before they begin a technical training regimen which takes nearly twice the time of the Israeli program. Results are comparable. There are several studies in the literature of industrial relations which compare prerequisites and training for certain specific jobs in Buffalo, New York, and, a few miles away, Ontario, Canada. Canadians achieve at least equal performance with much less stringent educational and licensing requirements. The movement toward expanded duties auxiliaries in law, medicine and dentistry illustrate this trend.

12. The inevitable consequence of this perspective is that the traditional compartments of knowledge are being demolished. The post-1950 personality derives satisfaction and security from being able to utilize knowledge as the ruling principle of accomplishment, not job titles, job descriptions, rigid boundaries of traditional disciplines or seniority.

13. All of the above is represented in two key attitudes of the post-1950 personalities which are diagnostically significant in separating them from their pre-1950 counterpart.

First — a deep conviction that opportunities for achievement, personal growth and an individual's values are inseparable and internalized. The pre-1950 personality is inclined to separate these same three aspects of life and believes that external circumstances greatly affect the outcome of each.

And second — a post-1950 personality finds that competence is potentially available to every person because it is seen as an amalgam of diverse abilities and sensitivities applied in a useful way to a felt need. The pre-1950 personality tends to think of competence as something which is certified by degree, experience and title; and which is not so much a possession as a right earned by the person who holds a suitable degree, experience and title.

14. In fact, the occidental world is becoming increasingly oriental in its values and philosophy. The Western world has traditionally seen the Creator and the created as separate and unequal. The created earn in some way (faith, good works) the privilege of participating in the goodness of the Creator. The Eastern world, however, in virtually all of its philosophies and religions, has taught that the Creator and the created are one; and that the Creator has endowed the created with the ability to recognize and act upon truth through self-discipline. This concept of oneness, of unity, is more and more evident in the post-1950 personality. Our cultural fascination with internalized forms of self-discipline (transcendental meditation, yoga, progressive relaxation, biofeedback) and the increasing influence of Eastern religions, particularly Zen Buddhism, on Western institutions and religions is neither transitory nor accidental.

15. Increasingly, we are coming to understand that much of what has historically been regarded as instinctual knowledge is, in fact, learned behavior. We seem to be light years away from knowing how to apply this knowledge. Yet within the next 20 years, this realization will probably rework our culture.

16. By age six, the average middle-class child has watched television for more than 6,000 hours. The child's primary education is increasingly influenced by electronic media. Thus, the post-1950 child has developed high skills in receiving information visually, orally and aurally, but the child's ability to communicate by written word is demonstrably deteriorating.

17. Largely as a result of television, post-1950 personalities have an awareness, a worldview, which pre-1950 people do not have. Similarly, post-1950 children comprehend time and distance in a very different way than their earlier counterparts. After all, they've seen the moon, Mars and every nation on earth. Today's children grow up in a world where walking on the moon is ordinary and expected.

18. On a cosmological level, the same thing holds. Young children have an acceptance of the universe and our infinitely small place in it which their elders do not have and often find intimidating.

19. The post-1950 personality has a self-discovered hesitancy, perhaps even a contempt, for objectivity; and a deep abiding belief that at its core, objectivity is essentially subjective. Much of what we are learning from perceptual psychology confirms this notion. Furthermore, there are now ample data to show that

unimpeachable investigators of high integrity are subjectively influenced in the taking of objective measurements. (During the late 1960s, prior to laboratory automation, I was able to demonstrate that when medical technicians were personally fond of a physician and they possessed informal knowledge of his presumptive diagnosis, their laboratory tests tended to confirm that diagnosis. When they did not care for the physician, the results they found tended to counter his diagnosis.)

20. Clearly, the attitudes we have described are at once both cause and effect of the way we culturally value work. It is not surprising, therefore, that pre-1950 people tend to regard work as the inevitable cost of a comfortable existence in what they perceive as the real world. Post-1950 workers increasingly display confidence that work is a natural, not a required, condition; that the worker has the right to expect joy, fulfillment and satisfaction from work, not merely survival or physical comfort; and because work is natural, the rules of work should be internally generated and self-applied. The post-1950 worker is much more committed to task attainment than satisfying a time requirement. The requirements of knowledge and fulfillment of participatory objectives are more meaningful than seniority or arbitrarily derived decisions by authority figures.

In all of these respects, the pre-1950 worker tends to be different. Work/not work/play activities are properly separate and are defined by some aspect of time: Time of day, time of year, vacation time, weekend time, etc. Clocks, calendars, schedules and fixed plans are deemed to be important. The pre-1950 worker usually believes that seniority and authority are valid determinants of both values and judgment-making. The enjoyment of work is not expected; when it happens, the pre-1950 personality is grateful for what he considers a short-term respite. On-going enjoyment is looked upon as neurotic behavior or evidence that nothing of consequence is being accomplished.

Our culture's changing attitude toward work is probably the most basic and socially significant shift of values now underway. The metamorphosis of the work ethic affects (and will ultimately transform) every cultural institution (including churches and schools, not just offices and factories). That is why one commentator, Peter Drucker, has referred to the changing work ethic as "the keystone of tomorrow".

IN SUMMARY: OUR PERCEPTION OF WORK DETERMINES OUR PERCEPTION OF OURSELVES.

21. In a discussion of human rights, it is important to the post-1950 personality that the rights of women, or any other special group, are not disenfranchised by having separate rights defined for them. Thus, the rights of women in the minds of post-1950 personalities are neither more nor less than human rights which are equally applied to women.

The advent of reliable, inexpensive, safe means of contraception have given women ownership of their biology. Their entry into the labor market — not out of economic or social need but personal satisfaction — is immensely important to the post-1950 person. Some of the consequences include later marriages; smaller families; more childless couples; postponement of conception to later years; innovative application of child-rearing philosophies — especially variations of the Israeli kibbutz; and a strong need to be involved in the care of their own bodies rather than being the objects of an industrialized, male-dominated medical apparatus.

22. One further manifestation of human rights is seen in the radicalization of the Anglo-Saxon judicial process. The 1954 landmark decision (Brown *vs* USA) of the Supreme Court (in which the court determined that otherwise equal schools which segregated pupils by race are not equal) was the first major decision in our entire judicial history which departed from case law, *i.e.*, legal precedent. Prior to this decision, all judicial rulings were deductively applied interpretation of prior decisions. But in this decision, for the first time the court utilized non-judicial determinations — specifically the research of a Swedish sociologist, Gunner Myrdal. Legal reasoning is the quintessence of the deductive method; for extra-legal and non-deductive material to have been introduced at the highest level into the judicial process is significant beyond all easy grasp.

What we call the beginning is often the end. And to make the end is to make a beginning. The end is where we start from.

T. S. Eliot

Chapter IX

THE NEW PARADIGM

"I had an apartment in Cambridge that was filled with antiques and I gave charming dinner parties. I had a Mercedes Benz sedan and a Triumph motorcycle and a Cessna airplane and an MG sportscar and a sailboat and a bicycle. I regularly vacationed in the Caribbean where I did scuba diving…..

"Here was my predicament. I was a social scientist but I was not really a scholar. I came out of a Jewish anxiety-ridden, high-achieving tradition. Though I had been through five years of psychoanalysis, still, every time I lectured, I would get extraordinary diarrhea. I could study ten hours and prepare a really good lecture on Freud or human motivation. But it was all behind a wall. It was theoretical. I theorized this or I theorized that. I espoused ideas and intellectual concepts that were quite separate from my own experience …. I could serve on government committees … have grants … travel … sit on doctoral committees but there was still a horrible awareness that I didn't know enough to make it all fall together. I wondered if I was going to spend the next forty years not knowing. The whole thing was too empty. It was not honest."

These words are taken from Ram Dass's remarkable book, *Remember Now Be Here*. It speaks deeply to feelings which many of us have — even if we are not quite ready to recognize or acknowledge them.

It is bit of a cliché to suggest that we are in the midst of an enormous paradigm shift, perhaps the most consequential shift in the recorded history of the world. I am one of many who, over the years, have written extensively about this new paradigm, and every university library is filled with books that explore the phenomenon which we are now living.

Based on my consultative work with many clients, I observe there are *apparently* well-settled people who seem to be experiencing a sense of profound upheaval in their lives. Anxiety is a common bed-fellow. Many seem to be enduring a disruption of an established order, and they are sensing a quality of change which, somehow, is deeper and darker than they remember from the stories of their parents.

Often I work with people who report they are surrounded by a malevolent energy that is discontinuous, unpredictable and severe. Perhaps they feel not only a loss of direction but, even more unsettling, a disruption of continuity. For many, there is an aura of inevitability to a corrosive process which is eating away at their personal autonomy and effectiveness.

Traditional aspirations seem more brittle and less relevant. Many are discovering what they perceive as New Rules. They feel the effects of the rules. But the Rule Book isn't available and so they live with a nagging suspicion that it's not yet been written. Because the Old Rules are no longer reliable, they wonder whether an optimal life of choice is possible. As their sense of confidence and optimism is dissolved, it's easy for them to become fearful, cynical, withdrawn and depressed.

Let me share a paragraph from a letter which I received some years ago. The writer is a dear friend who, by the external standards admired by the world, would be deemed "successful". Here is what he said:

> I wish it were possible for my children to grow up in a world where hard work, honesty, excellence and service would assure their happiness and prosperity. That world existed when I was a boy. But it has mostly disappeared. The rules are changing. It's as though the Commissioner of the NFL stopped the Super Bowl mid-way into the third quarter to announce that effective immediately a touchdown would be awarded only four points, and that the field would be lengthened by 20 yards.

From time to time I return to a book which was first published in 1981. The title is *Voluntary Simplicity: Toward a Way of Life that is Outwardly Simple, Inwardly Rich*. The author is Duane Elgin. The first half of the book is in the grand tradition of Spangler and Toynbee. Elgin quotes with admiration these words from Toynbee's *A Study of History*: "A growing civilization may be defined as one in which the components of its culture are in harmony with each other and form an integral whole. A disintegrating civilization can be defined as one in which these same elements have fallen into discord."

Elgin believes that Western industrial civilization is following a four-part cycle.

Stage I is "an era of faith" in which there was "high social consensus and a strong sense of shared social purpose... Bureaucratic complexity was low and activities were largely self-regulated."

Stage II is "an era of reason" during which there was a slow weakening of consensus and purpose. Bureaucratic complexity increased and so activities were becoming much more regulated."

Stage III is "an era of cynicism" marked by weakened consensus and fragmentation. The demands of special interest groups became much stronger. Bureaucratic organizations took on a life of their own; the rapidity of their growth exceeded the capacity of managers to direct and meaningfully regulate their activities.

Stage IV is "an era of despair" during which there is a collapse of consensus. Society is marked by multiple and conflicting social purposes. Bureaucratic complexity overwhelms the functioning of cultural institutions. There is a disintegration of established ways and values. In 1981 Elgin predicted that by the mid 1990s, the USA and Canada would be Stage IV societies "characterized by disharmony, discord, dis-synchronization and marked fragmentation."

Today there is considerable visible evidence of what Elgin referred to as Stage IV. Attitudes, beliefs and values are changing more rapidly than their institutional representations. Because ideas change prior to their institutional representation, the result is discordance as those who are empowered by new ideas must confront others who are committed to the preservation of old institutions. While some values may be preserved and extended, they are expressed so differently that they become unacceptable to the guardians of the old institutions.

Emile Durkheim, who wrote at the turn of the century, deserves to be remembered as the father of the then new science of sociology. His study of the cultural factors relating to suicide is widely admired, even today, for both its content and methodology. He introduced a useful word, *anomie*. Its ancient Greek roots give the word a literal meaning of "without order" or "without organization". In the literature of sociology, the word refers to a society which has lost its sense of communal meaning. Through the dissolution of social structure, cultural norms and moral imperatives are put into disarray.

In the presence of cultural anomie, individuals feel a loss of orientation. They experience themselves as aimless and impotent. Aspirations and purpose deteriorate as challenges of existence and survival absorb the human energy which would otherwise be available for investment in autonomy, enlighten-ment, creativity and beauty.

It's important to realize that anomie is a cultural pheno-menon which influences individual behavior. *Notice, also, the idea of living by intent is precisely contrary to anomie.* When we lose our self-perceived capacity to organize life around personally optimal choices, we are inclined to seek relationships with others who are similarly encumbered. This is true in the workplace and in our personal lives. Here is an example of "like" attracting "like"; or, if you prefer, dysfunctional people feeling more comfortable with others who share their dysfunction. Common sense and simple observation confirm that dysfunctional people tend to bond with others based upon their mutual anxieties and fears. (Functional people bond with each other based on their abundant sense of what is possible.) Here is precisely why dysfunctional organizations are not static; they continually tend to move toward more serious levels of dysfunction.

> [Please note that "dysfunction", as here used, is a descriptive term, not a moral or clinical judgment. Functional people are able to move toward their highest, most pure aspirations while dysfunctional people seem to unconsciously subvert their own becoming.]

The rigid imposition of expectations, whether by an individual or a group, represents a debilitating form of control which inevitably leads to the preservation and extension of the *status quo*.

Here is the rub: *Organizations do not grow except as a function of the growth of individuals within the organization. But since individuals tend to bond based upon shared fears and anxieties, it is extremely difficult for organizational structure and climate to meaningfully change. Indeed, such change is impossible except in the presence of a vision which will attract the commitment of at least a few individuals.*

In summary, whether we are talking about a marriage, a family, a church or school, a business/professional office or a factory, organizational growth is always, always, always an extension of individual growth.

As I discussed in an earlier chapter, vision involves possibilities rather than probabilities. Vision is a manifestation of optimal choice, not reactive acceptance. Most of you will likely agree that we are in the midst of a paradigm shift. But I am suggesting that as an aspect of this paradigm shift, we are witnesses to the emergence of a plausible new vision for our culture. Moreover, I believe there is growing evidence that this new vision is now being felt, consciously or pre-consciously, by many people.

The phrase "paradigm shift" entered our language with the publication in 1962 of Thomas Kuhn's important book, *The Structure of Scientific Revolutions*. A paradigm is much more than a model. It is an organizing principle at the very core of society which sponsors transformational change. *This is a deep process which is beyond our ability to manipulate or control. However, the outcome of the process will be influenced by our perceptions, intentions, choices and behaviors.* One of Kuhn's most attentive readers was the physicist, Fritjof Capra, who offered a definition of paradigm which is lucid and useful: "*A paradigm is a constellation of concepts, values, perceptions and practices shared by a community, and which form a particular vision of reality that provides a community with a continuing basis for organizing itself.*"

I hope you will find credence in my belief that we already have begun to experience the emergence of new cultural values. In recent years I have read perhaps half a hundred summaries of these emerging values, and I have found important insights in many of them. Allow me to offer a brief summary of the summaries:

A shift from "outer" to "inner" authority. The old paradigm was causality-centered and authority-based. It relied upon an outside/in process. The new paradigm recognizes and trusts the validity of inner sources of knowing.

A shift from "parts" to "whole". In the old paradigm, it was assumed that the dynamics of the whole could best be understood and appreciated by studying the characteristics of the parts. In the new paradigm, the relationship between the parts and the whole is reversed. Today we are realizing that the characteristics of the parts cannot be grasped except through an appreciative understanding of the dynamics of the whole.

A shift from "disease" to "health and wellness". The old paradigm corrected or cured deviations from quantifiable norms, an outside/in, authoritarian procedure. The new paradigm accepts and supports our innate capacity to heal, an inside/out process in which attitudes drive physiology. This new paradigm involves active participation and co-discovery rather than the passive acceptance of external therapeutic intervention.

A shift from "separateness" to "integration". The old paradigm established limits, boundaries and definitions which evoked separateness and isolation. The new paradigm provides a cosmic sense of relationship in which everything is related to and has an effect on everything else.

A shift from "finite" to "infinite". Ultimately, there are no parts at all. As I will discuss later, everything is fundamentally insubstantial energy, and what we call a "part" is merely a pattern of an inseparable, never-ending web of systematic relationships. Whether we are talking about a cosmic universe or a sub-nuclear particle, everything is composed of "parts" and, simultaneously, everything is part of a larger whole.

A shift from "hyper-individualism" to "community". The old paradigm was based on the Horatio Alger story and the egocentric belief that one person could provide the pivot for a whole enterprise. The new paradigm suggests that all of us are more competent and powerful than any of us. But each of us has an innate opportunity to facilitate leadership, and this leadership can provoke a vision which will become the core of a community.

A shift from "dirt, rock and water" to the organic concept of "Gaia". The old paradigm looked upon Planet Earth as a "thing" which could be analyzed and used. But the new paradigm sees Planet Earth as a complex organic living system. The idea of Gaia is founded upon the belief that the planet itself is alive, and is more than its geology.

A shift from "centralized" to "a-centric" power. Movement is away from hierarchy, precedent and control (the old paradigm) toward a reliance on networking, self-discovery and shared learning.

A shift from a "causal-based universe" to a "holographic universe". We are inculturated to believe that every event in the universe can be understood causally, and that each event has its own integrity. *But now we are beginning to appreciate that in every event we can see the whole of the universe (which is, of course, the functional essence of a*

167

hologram). This is profoundly important because in a causal universe if I do "X", then only "Y" is influenced. But in a holographic universe, if I do "X" my behavior, in some manner and degree, is influencing every aspect of the whole. Thus the power of the individual (for better or worse) is enhanced enormously. It is the difference between 1+1+1+1=4 as compared to 4 to the 4th power.

A shift from "mechanistic" to "living" systems. The old paradigm created models based on mechanistic assumptions and systems. The new paradigm creates models which manifest an acceptance of the principles and processes that are associated with living (organic) systems.

A shift from strategies based on "competition" to strategies based on the principles of "healing, reconciliation and partnership". The old paradigm insisted on winners and losers. The new paradigm acknowledges the possibility and desirability of all participants realizing a beneficial gain.

A shift from "structure" to "process". The old paradigm taught us that there are fundamental structures in nature, and that these structures interact as a result of forces and mechanisms which give rise to processes. But in the new paradigm, all structure is seen as a momentary manifestation of an underlying process. Thus, for example, "death" and "life" are not separate and opposite; they are different representations of the same whole. We are coming to understand that when we focus only on structure, we cannot understand underlying processes. Process, not structure, is foundational, and structure has no meaning or integrity except as a manifestation of process.

A shift from "etiology" to "phenomenology". The old paradigm taught that understanding required knowledge of etiology which, in turn, is derived from the discovery of causality. The new paradigm is more concerned with how a person experiences an event, and the meaning an individual finds in it, rather than what has caused the event.

A shift from "objective" science to "epistemic" science. In the old paradigm, scientific descriptions were believed to be objective. These descriptions, when properly rendered, were independent of the human observer and the processes of knowledge. The new paradigm is derived from epistemology, the name classically given to that discipline of formal philosophy which is concerned with the investigation of the nature and origin of knowledge. For example, it has been conclusively demonstrated that merely the act of observing sub-atomic particles causes their physical behavior to change.

Thus, any description of sub-atomic particles must be epistemological since *how* we observe these particles alters *what* we see. It follows, therefore, that science is not objective; it is subjective. That is, science is influenced, albeit subtly, by the scientist.

A shift from "total truth" to "approximate description". The old paradigm is based on the absolute certainty of scientific knowledge. The new paradigm acknowledges that all scientific concepts, theories, definitions and explanations are, *by their intrinsic nature*, limited, approximate and tentative. *A system cannot simultaneously be valid and complete.* If valid, the system is evolving in response to its environment and so it is not complete. If it is complete, then it is static and, therefore, invalid. This was mathematically demonstrated in what has come to be known in logic as Gödel's Proof.

A shift from "material reality" to "immaterial reality". The old paradigm excelled at the discovery, definition and manipulation of form and substance. That which lacked form and substance was not "real". But in the new paradigm, we are coming to appreciate that reality is not to be found in either form or substance since form and substance are illusionary... meaning un-real. What is *really* real has neither form nor substance.

A shift from "modular organization" to "network organization". Since the origin of rigorous science thousands of years ago in Egypt, we have communicated scientific knowledge through a sequential and additive process of laws, principles, postulates, corollaries and applications. The new paradigm is not sequential. Fixed and sequential modularity is being displaced by a dynamic flow of networking. As we begin to perceive that all of physical reality is a network of relationships, we readily see how everything relates to everything.

A shift from "domination and control" to "cooperation and coordination". Throughout the development of the scientific method, we had more and more opportunities to apply what were deemed to be scientific truths. An underlying assumption was that through the knowledge gained with the scientific method, humans were destined to both control and dominate nature. The new paradigm seeks to achieve a harmonious whole through the cooperative coordination of the parts. Harmony replaces hierarchy. Equilibrium displaces force. Balance eliminates domination.

A *shift from "hierarchy" to "collegiality"*. We can formally define a hierarchy by this logic chain: *When A is more than B and B is more than C, then A is more than C.* Notice, please, that this logic chain is linear and fixed. The process of this logic chain is central to the way that most of us have experienced our schools, churches, families and, as adults, the workplace.

But there is another kind of logic that leads us toward collegiality. Here the logic chain has a much different dynamic … and a much different outcome. *When A is more than B and B is more than C, then C is potentially more than A.* "How can that be?" you might be asking. Of course, the only way this can happen is when the model is circular and enfolding.

Collegiality is a mode of organization in which form, function and responsibilities are situationally defined by participants, each of whom spontaneously gives to and receives from the others. The criterion is simple: *At the present moment and in this current situation, what utilization of organizational resources will best facilitate our vision?*

Hierarchy is based upon title, formalized job descriptions and a belief that commands move from the top down while information moves from the bottom up. Collegiality rejects this fixed linearity in favor of a values-based, mission-driven model which always has continuing feedback exchanges with context and environment.

A shift from "responsibility for outcome" to "responsibility for input". As your spouse, employer, employee or friend, I cannot accept responsibility for your outcome. The reason, of course, is that your outcome will be influenced by a myriad of factors which are quite beyond my control. However, I *am* able to accept responsibility for *me*.

A shift from "limited" to "unlimited" access of information. In the old paradigm, availability of information was defined organizationally by my need to know. And, generally, my need to know was defined by title and seniority. But the new paradigm supports me in seeking information simply because I want to have it. I am organizationally rewarded for my desire to have information, and my access is not limited by title or seniority.

When I use newly acquired information in ways that advance the organizational vision, my responsibilities and opportunities expand. Were I to misuse the information (which includes not using it), then I would not be facilitating the vision and so my behavior would be inappropriate.

A shift from "scarcity" to "abundance". The old paradigm implied scarcity; resources were seen as limited and had to be wrestled from nature and life experiences. The new paradigm is abundant; it looks upon the universe as providing a constantly expanding, infinitely renewable resource — knowledge. And through the sensible use of this resource, all other resources become available and plentiful.

A shift from "doctrine-based religion" to "shared spirituality". In the old paradigm, historically derived doctrines and dogma were used to define the separateness of religions and their institutions. In the new paradigm, there is a shared vision of spirituality which is the common heritage of all people, regardless of the individual religious expressions which a person may choose.

A shift from "maintenance learning" to "innovative learning". The old paradigm primarily advocated what Warren Bennis called "maintenance learning", i.e., the acquisition of fixed outlooks, methods and rules for dealing with known and recurring situations. It is a type of learning designed to maintain an existing system or an established way of life. Current performance is compared only with past performance, never with what might have been or what is yet to be. Innovative learning focuses upon preparing people and organizations to deal effectively with new situations. This requires the anticipation of environments that have not yet appeared. There is no familiar context within which innovative learning can take place. Indeed, the construction of new contexts is part of innovative learning.

○ ○ ○

Surely this list is not complete. But it provides you with a perspective of what I believe is occurring. And it represents a matrix that will ultimately hold the new prevailing attitudes of our emerging culture. There is considerable evidence of a new world vision that is filled with fresh possibilities and promises. I submit that uncounted millions of people, certainly including many who are not formally well educated, have an intuitive sense that their culture is changing and, on some level, they are already coming to feel a comforting resonance with what is emerging.

Truly, living by intent is an idea whose time has come. Within this new paradigm, the principles and processes of living by intent are natural, congruent and effective. To recognize what is happening is to provide ourselves with an extraordinary opportunity to thrive.

Everyone takes the limits of his own
vision for the limits of the world.

Arthur Schopenhauer

Chapter X

VISION: HOW THE "*IMPROBABLE*" HELP US TO ATTAIN THE "*IMPOSSIBLE*"

"What do you mean by vision?" a reader of an early draft of this chapter asked me. Here is my response:

A vision is your imaginative definition of a life of intent, a life which supports you in seeking your most pure aspirations. A life that feeds your soul by providing opportunities for you to serve others in ways that are deeply meaningful. A life which encourages you to feel whole, complete and always in process of becoming more than you are. A vision represents your most noble and least distorted sense of self.

A vision is not unreal; a vision is the essence of what *is* real.

While achieving a vision may not be probable, it *is* possible. The more nearly you attain your vision, the more likely it is that you will always be in process of redefining it. *That's because your vision is a real-world representation of your spirit and soul which, by definition, are fields of energy that are always responding to what is surrounding you.* The more clearly you see your vision, the more you realize that within yourself is an infinite array of possibilities.

Thus — vision is a necessary precursor to a life of intent.

Over the years I've discussed the idea of "mental models". All of us carry mental models in our heads, probably hundreds of them. A mental model is an assumption, usually an unconscious assumption, which represents a learned and automatic response to a situation. Typically we are unaware of the derivation of our mental models and how they are currently functioning in our lives. Mental models tend to be murky, ill-defined and often ambiguous. But they are very, very real and impactful!

Mental models are not "bad" or "good". The significance of mental models is behavioral, not moral. In fact, they are a necessary and inevitable aspect of enculturation. *However, we can choose to become more aware of our mental models and more sensitive to the ways in which they have historically guided us in our decision-making. When we choose to begin an examination of our mental models, we are helping ourselves to become visionary and, thereby, to live more intentionally.* Let me say this another way: As we become aware of the constraints which we impose on ourselves, what I here calling our mental models, we are better able to become free to visualize a life of intent.

When I talk with my clients about the formulation of a personal vision, I tell them that a vision *cannot* be practical, feasible or affordable. That is a shocking and improbable statement which strikes many people as irresponsible.

But it is clearly valid. Our unexamined mental models determine for us — unthoughtfully and probably unconsciously — what we deem to be practical, feasible and affordable.

The eagle of our imagination cannot soar if it must carry the weight of these mental models. When we hold our vision-making to what we *now* regard as practical, feasible and affordable, our new vision turns out to be remarkably similar to the qualities of life that we are presently experiencing.

In his wonderful book, *Zen and the Art of Motorcycle Maintenance*, Robert Pirsig reminds us that "... if a factory is torn down but the rationality which produced it is left standing, then that rationality will simply produce another factory." When I say that a vision cannot be practical, feasible or affordable, I'm also telling you that a vision cannot be rational. A vision must be supra-rational if it is to displace Pirsig's factory.

I am not arguing in favor of irresponsibility. As part of vision-making and strategic planning, there are processes by which we learn to deal effectively with questions of practicality, feasibility and affordability. *But vision-making cannot begin with these considerations. First we must let our eagle soar.*

The most difficult challenge I face in my consulting practice is to help my clients soar *irresponsibly* on the wings of their imagination. There are at least two explanations for why this is a difficult challenge. First — we are all products of a culture which, subtly and overtly, praise us and reward us for "being responsible". Second — since being responsible is "good", then being irresponsible is "bad" and so we sink into the muck of a moralistic swamp rather than recognizing that the issue (and the only issue!) is strategic, not moralistic. The issue is not good/bad. It is instead our deeply personal desire to answer from the depth of our soul Dan Millman's brilliant question, "How good can you stand it?" Notice, please, that Millman's question is strongly counter-cultural. Traditionally we would ask, "How bad can you stand it? How much pain can you endure? How tough are you?"

As you can see, vision-making involves qualitative processes. The distinction between "qualitative" and "quantitative" is pivotal. If "X" can be added, subtracted, multiplied, divided, compared or measured, then by definition it is quantitative. If "X" is not quantitative, then it is qualitative.

Notice, please, everything that's quantitative involves cognition and materiality. By contrast everything that is qualitative involves affect (feelings) and imagination (immateriality). *The beginning of vision-making must always, always, always be a qualitative process.* If it is even a little bit quantitative, then the outcome will not be visionary. This is an absolute and non-negotiable condition. It can be no other way.

As an early introduction to vision-making (and ultimately to strategic planning), I frequently ask my clients to answer this question, "What are the feelings that you would like to have more of?" This is a highly strategic question. When it is answered thoughtfully, my client is also defining those feelings which s/he wants to have less represented. Thus, when a client says to me, "I would like more tranquility in my life", clearly the client is also saying, "I would like to have less hassle in my life".

My experience over many years tells me that it is difficult — sometimes profoundly difficult — to facilitate my client in identifying these positive feelings. Important and often primal mental models may intrude.

This is not a theoretical exercise. For example, as I come to know my client, I might ask: "Does this set of behaviors which you are now describing increase or intensify the feelings that you want more of?" Or my client might share an expectation: "I think it makes sense for me to . . . ." And I might then ask, "How will that help you to have more of the feelings that you want?" Processing these questions is a powerful experience.

By focusing on the affirmation of those feelings that my client wants to have more fully represented in his/her life, we begin to move beyond the fixed but invisible logic systems (or mental models) that historically have caused my client to accept the bondage of "probabilities" (which are quantitative and cognitive) and to seek the freedom inherent in "possibilities" (which are qualitative and affective). This is an subtle but awesome shift. An exploration of what is possible will inevitably move toward what is visionary. *In the absence of possibilities, there cannot be a vision. Probabilities are vision-killing.*

Frequently a client wants to reject the idea of possibilities in order to discuss an economic consideration. That which is quantifiable carries an aura of probability and, thereby, comfort, and so this is understandable. But my experience is that economic issues are hardly ever the problem. Typically they are a symptom of a problem, usually an unrecognized problem, that, in turn, is the result of a constellation of unseen but constraining mental models.

The process by which a client gains this realization is *not* analytic, at least in the conventional sense. The origin and derivation of these mental models is much less important, certainly in the beginning, than helping a client to gain a dynamic appreciation of the positive feelings s/he would like to more abundantly have in the here-and-now.

By learning to focus on positive feelings, a client moves closer to a vision of a preferred future. *The creation of a vision is a sublime act of affirmation and optimism.* Thus, a genuine commitment to create a personal vision is itself a decision with enormous life-changing potential.

Please let me share in full William Faulkner's acceptance when in 1949 he received the Nobel Laureate in Literature. I offer you his statement because it is an elegant example of a vision statement. The affirming optimism permeates the soul of even the most casual reader.

Our tragedy today is a general and universal physical fear so long sustained by now that we can even bear it. There are no longer problems of the spirit. There is only the question: When will I be blown up? Because of this, the young man or woman writing today has forgotten the problems of the human heart in conflict with itself. He must learn them again. He must teach himself that the basest of all things is to be afraid; and, teaching himself that, forget it forever, leaving no room in his workshop for anything but the old verities and truths of the heart. Until he does so, he labors under a curse. He writes not of love but of lust, of defeats in which nobody loses anything of value, of victories without hope and, worst of all, without pity or compassion. His griefs grieve on no universal bones, having no scars. He writes not of the heart but of the glands.

Until he relearns these things, he will write as though he stood alone and watched the end of man. I decline to accept the end of man. It is easy enough to say that man is immortal simply because he will endure; that when the last ding-dong of doom has clanged and faded from the last worthless rock hanging tideless in the last red and dying evening, that even then there will still be one more sound: that of his puny inexhaustible voice, still talking. I refuse to accept this. I believe that man will not merely endure; he will prevail.

Because of the time at which Faulkner delivered these remarks, many who read them felt that his reference to "a general and universal physical fear" was prompted by the "Cold War" and the growing threat of a nuclear disaster. I don't know whether that is correct. But I do know Faulkner was belligerently a-political and I choose to believe that the physical fear he refers to is existentially related to the human condition. I believe that his statement is more than eloquent and beautiful. It is an exquisitely optimistic declaration which is valid today and will be no less valid in a hundred years.

Vision-making is an affirming, intensely optimistic and entirely appropriate acknowledgment of our human potential and our spiritual energy. That has always been true. But today the importance of vision may be historically unique.

The window of opportunity is open. No decision is a decision. The choice is yours.

We are afraid to become that which we glimpse in our most perfect moments, under the most perfect conditions, when we are realizing the greatest courage. We enjoy and even thrill to the god-like possibilities we see in ourselves during such peak moments. And yet we simultaneously shiver with weakness, awe and fear before these same possibilities.

Abraham Maslow

Chapter XI

MORALITY AS A VISIONARY IMPERATIVE

My purpose is to demonstrate that moral behavior *must* be visionary; and, conversely, the generation of a vision is inevitably a moral exercise. I want to begin by bringing to your attention the brilliant and important book, *Revolt of the Masses*, written by Ortega y Gassett and published in 1929. The logic of his book is rigorous. His sense of history is pure. The vision of the book is powerful. And the applicability of his argument is timeless and universal. It surely deserves a place on anyone's list of the most important books of the 20th century.

Ortega y Gassett's use of the word "mass" is important. He is not merely referring to a numeric headcount. Instead — his idea of mass carries three crucial characteristics:

> *First* — deterioration of internal social structure,
>
> *Second* — lack of an integrating tradition and
>
> *Third* — the absence of a shared vision of a preferred future.

Gassett (and, later, Hannah Arendt in her *The Origins of Totalitarianism*) help us to understand that when a group does not have an *acknowledged* set of operative values, there is *always* an erosion of individual autonomy and freedom and, simultaneously, an enhanced potential for group members to abandon their individual decision-making to others. *Clearly, massification leads to an abdication of self-responsibility. By definition, this is immoral because, psychologically and spiritually, it is a denial of free will and a denial of intent.*

The consequences of massification adversely influence all groups — certainly families, business entities, churches and political/governmental constellations. Let me say this another way: The three characteristics of mass as identified by Gassett encourage people to assign their individuality to what George Orwell called groupthink which, Orwell argues, leads to the tyranny of a charismatic self-serving leader.

As I discussed in an prior chapter, an earlier perspective of this phenomenon was described a century ago by Emile Durkheim, a French sociologist whose trenchant observations and contextual methodology provide the foundation for much contemporary sociological research. Within the behavioral sciences he was the first to describe *anomie*. The ancient Greek root gives the word a literal meaning of "without order" or "without organization".

Sociologically, the word refers to a society which has lost its sense of community, generally as a result of the dissolution of social structure. In the absence of community, there is a related loss of both cultural norms and moral order. In the presence of *anomie*, members of society feel aimless and ineffective — even impotent. As cultural purpose and meaning atrophy, there is a withering of personal planning and ambition. Existential questions of survival absorb human energy which otherwise might be available for investment in aspirations, enlightenment, creativity, beauty and nobility. *Thus — we can think of* anomie *as an inevitable outcome of Gassett's mass.*

Gassett's three characteristics of mass are now clearly evident in our society. And *anomie* has so infiltrated our culture that many regard the social aimlessness of *anomie* as expected and, therefore, normal. I disagree. We must realize that *anomie* places our freedom of choice and autonomy in severe jeopardy. Emphatically, while this may be statistically "normal", it is not "normal" and, as we shall see, it is not moral.

Consider the consequences of *anomie* for a moment; I think you will agree that it is a major impediment to meaningful relationships. An individual who cannot accept responsibility for personal choices will establish relationships that are superficial, inauthentic and, ultimately, degrading. This, in turn, saps the cohesion (and, therefore, the effectiveness) of all organizational structures. *This process is insidious.* A multinational corporation employing 200,000 is as much at risk as a small professional office with a staff of five or a family of three.

But there is more to be said. The absence of cultural purpose and structure creates situations in which individuals tend to move toward relationships that will tolerate (or even enhance) their dysfunction. As these individuals become less effective, they also blunt the effectiveness of the groups in which they are members. There is a perpetuation of disintegration marked by "subtractive synergy" whereby more and more of anything (people, rules, organizational structure) become less and less functional, especially as the Law of the Least Common Denominator is activated by their collective failures.

The *absence* of choice becomes the *denial* of choice. Social and cultural values are degraded. Personal initiative is experienced as rude, even obnoxious. Since in this environment an individual no longer accepts responsibility for self, personal behavior (and, therefore, personal morality) becomes irrelevant. Nobility of hope is displaced by simple maintenance of basic biology.

Notice, please, that *anomie* is contrary to vision. A vision expands and enriches a sense of what is possible. Whether the vision belongs to a person or a group of people, it becomes a creative expression of what can be. *Anomie*, however, is a process of disintegration and degradation.

In summary: Vision exists in the future; *anomie* creates people and groups who see themselves as future-less ... without history, continuity or purpose.

On the level of the individual and the family, the city, state/province and nation, we lack a respectful awareness of the traditions which in an earlier day helped us to maintain an integrated sense of presence. Individually and in our groupings, we suffer from a deterioration of social structure, and so we are inclined to act in ways that do not contribute to an enduring sense of purpose and meaning. Mass leads to *anomie*; and *anomie* causes social fragmentation and erosion of meaning in ordinary affairs of life. In this circumstance, the idea of living by intent feels unreal, impractical and even subversive.

Living by intent and groupthink are absolutely contrary and antagonistic. Living by intent *requires* equality of opportunity while also honoring the possibility of inequality of outcome. Both of these opportunities are in contradiction to groupthink. Mass has lead us to a perversion of equality in which each of us is deemed to be the same as all of us. We are "dumbed down" to the mean. Since all of us are the same, we should expect the same.

As the prophet Isaiah noted some 800 years before the birth of Christ, living without a vision is a risky business. That is especially true during a time of rapid, unpredictable and discontinuous change. Over the past 30 years, I have repeatedly suggested that we are living during such a period … and that the rapidity and discontinuity of change are still accelerating.

Perhaps the most crucial moral issue of our day is the existence of an economically mighty, politically powerful culture which has lost line-of-sight vision with its North Star. We experience the issues related to *anomie* as worldly, realistic and here-and-now; the immediacy of these issues encourages us to think about them without piety. And so it's easy to deny that these issues are moral issues. But emphatically they are!

We arrived at this sorry state because of subtle cultural endorsement of a series of implied equivalencies:

Average = Normal

Normal = Desirable

Desirable = Correct

Correct = Just

Just = Moral

Let me offer this definition of morality: *Generalized and acknowledged truths which help us to discern standards of righteous behavior.* I understand, of course, that morality is not ordinarily part of our workplace discussion. But I would like to suggest that a discussion of morality is extremely practical ... and that in today's world, the discussion cannot be avoided except at great cost to human and economic enterprise.

It's clear that morality is not something which we define for our own convenience. Indeed, there is a quality of timelessness about morality because the very idea of what is "moral" represents a distillation and application of wisdom gathered over considerable time.

But having said this, it is also true that throughout the ages (not just today), there have been different and conflicting perceptions of what is moral. Our society's current concern with assisted suicide is an example of how discussions of morality can require us to deal with ambiguity, paradox and uncertainty.

Let me give an example which over the years has had great personal meaning for me. Consider the agony described by the Lutheran minister, Dietrich Bonhoeffer, in the diary he kept while a prisoner of the Nazis. Perhaps you will remember his dilemma. As a Christian pastor, he was forbidden by Scripture and conscience to take a life. Yet over a three-year period he had come to acknowledge a *moral* obligation to participate in the assassination of Hitler, thereby hoping to preserve the lives of tens of thousands of Jews. Eventually he decided in favor of assassination by invoking what he called "the doctrine of the higher good". Bonhoeffer decided that he would best serve his God and his faith by participating knowingly in a forbidden act. (We know his story because his diary was smuggled out of Germany prior to Bonhoeffer's execution for his unsuccessful attempt on Hitler's life.)

Was this a "moral" choice? And how do we know? As you can see, discussions of morality can be extremely practical! Bonhoeffer's life — and his decision — illustrate that a moral act may not be popular, appreciated or even understood. Was Bonhoeffer an "average" man? Were his behaviors "normal"? Should we tell his story to our children because he acted in a "desirable" way? Was he "right" in what he did? Was he "just"? Is it appropriate for us to admire him as a "moral" person?

Let me return to the definition I offered you: *What is moral represents generalized and acknowledged truths that we use to help us in determining appropriate standards of righteous behavior.* If you will ponder this definition for a moment, I think you will agree that morality cannot be the result of tinkering. Morality is not achieved through a series of minor adjustments. We don't creep up on morality.

By definition, morality *is.* When we choose to live morally, we do so by doing so. We do not become moral through a series of modifications. We become moral by reason of choice and commitment.

Morality, which some regard as illusive and confusing, relates admirably to a concept which in the business world is clear-cut and definitive — what is often referred to as "breakaway thinking" or the older phrase, "strategic thinking". An operative definition will leap from the example below.

In 1988 a group of Australians surprised the world by winning the America's Cup sailing competition. The design of their boat's hull was controversial. It violated the expectations and the traditions of boat design. Because the official rules had never anticipated what the Australians did, it was not illegal. But in the minds of many, it should have been. After their victory, the team captain was interviewed by *Sports Illustrated* magazine. His words are crisp and clear. I clipped the article and have frequently quoted from it. Let me share a few sentences.

We came to realize that over the years we kept trying to make our boat a little bit better. To improve what we had done the year previous. But that never succeeded because the Americans were also trying to make their boat a little bit better. Since American resources allowed them to begin with a boat that already was a little bit better, we could never catch them. Our gain was offset by their gain. Once we grasped this, we knew that fine-tuning our hull design was inherently self-defeating. We needed a breakthrough.

I find great wisdom in his words. *As I consider my own life and the experiences of my clients, I've come to believe that a decision to improve a process or a behavior (fine-tuning) carries an implied commitment to retain it.* There is a world of difference between making the *status quo* better and breakaway (strategic) thinking. For example — when we intend to improve what is, inevitably we focus upon only a part of a whole. *But breakaway thinking demands a holistic perspective.* While refinement through fine-tuning causes us to isolate the parts of a system, breakaway thinking requires that we focus on the whole of a system and the integration of its parts.

In his worthy book, *Deep Change*, Robert E. Quinn further clarified the implication of breakaway thinking: "... change that is major in scope, discontinuous with the past and generally irreversible."

By fine-tuning, we minimize risk through a process of preservation/ conservation/maintenance. We keep what is ... what is known. But in breakaway thinking, we seek to overcome limits and limitations. We are searching for a new organizing principle. . . a new architecture. Here we are abandoning what is known. We open ourselves to possibilities . . . though at cost of probabilities.

Here, too, there is a provocative parallel between morality and breakaway thinking. When we exercise breakaway thinking, we are able to see ourselves in a future time frame discarding old patterns of behavior while creating newly congruent patterns. One serious consequence of breakaway thinking is that these new patterns often require us to reorder priorities and redefine objectives; when this happens, we must also prepare ourselves for the renegotiation of relationships.

Thus it is that morality — and a commitment to moral behavior — is a strategic and holistic decision. What is strategic is moral. What is immoral cannot be strategic.

I observe that there are a small set of factors which seem to suppress a person's capacity for breakaway thinking. And so it's not surprising to find that these same factors tend to support an individual's commitment to "fine-tuning".

First of all, often there is **a mosaic of fears**: an aversion to risk; fear of failure; fear of success; related fears of not measuring up to the expectations of another person. *These fears relate to how a person sees self, not to how a person sees the outside world.* Usually these perceptions have been legitimized by a person's early internalization of harsh, corrosive events and experiences. From time to time an individual may reactively develop a frozen harsh morality. But in my experience, this is usually an individual's way of protecting his/her vulnerability with a shield of apparent righteousness.

A second set of factors involves **feelings of personal powerlessness**. A perceived inability to make things happen in a way that is satisfying. Related feelings of hopelessness and helplessness.

A third set of factors involves a person's **inability to see the whole of the system which has been providing context for his/her life.** Sometimes I work with people who have never felt authorized to look beyond a specific set of tasks or functions. These people have a dim sense of their past … and only a vague appreciation of their potential for a self-determined future. Perhaps important parts of their system have been hidden or controlled by gatekeepers.

Sometimes there is a **disparity between functional requirements** (meet the payroll) **and a transcendent vision** (why are we here and whom do we serve).

There is not a hard line between these various factors … and while this listing is representative, it certainly is not complete. *But it suggests that the challenge of breakaway thinking (and moral behavior) is fundamentally a personal (not an organizational) challenge.* Yes, there are organizations which seek out and value those individuals with a capacity for innovation; just as there are organizations which repel them. But we must be clear that the prime source of creativity is within the individual's psyche and spirit, not the organizational matrix.

No organization can make an individual think strategically or act morally; nor can an organization prevent an individual from thinking strategically and acting morally.

Within the context of this argument, a decision to move toward a vision-based, mission-driven life of intent is a moral decision of the highest order. The challenge here goes beyond quality of life. The challenge for each of us is to create our lives as an artist would create a painting and, thereby, one-by-one, re-create the world.

Meaninglessness inhibits the fullness of life and can, therefore, be equated with illness; meaningfulness makes a great many things endurable, perhaps everything.

Carl G. Jung

Chapter XII

ADULT DEVELOPMENT AND THE PROGRESSION OF FAITH AND VISION

As we have seen in the prior two chapters, the creation of a vision is an act of optimism. Spiritual deprivation generates pessimism and, thereby, assures the absence of vision. Because vision is transcendent, the essence of vision is faith. Faith is inseparable from optimism. In the absence of faith, the possibility of transcendence is nil; without faith, we inevitably experience pessimism.

But what does "faith" mean, and how does it relate to vision? Are there aspects of morality that influence the intensity and magnitude of vision?

Let me refer you to a remarkable book by the American theologian, James W. Fowler. His title is precisely descriptive: *Stages of Faith — The Psychology of Human Development and the Quest for Meaning.*

Historically, human development has referred to the development of infants and children. But psychologists are coming to understand that human development is a lifelong process. In this sense, "human development" means something more than "learning from experience". The study of adult development involves the reorganization of psychic structure. While certainly this process is stimulated by life experiences, adult human development is an exploration of why and how adults create new inner paradigms for themselves and how these paradigms evolve. Nowhere is this clearer than in the adult's potential for continuing moral development.

In chapter eleven I had defined morality as "generalized and acknowledged truths which help us to discern standards of righteous behavior." The question I am now raising is whether people of good faith and high moral standards can disagree about what constitutes "righteous behavior". This is not a trivial question. If you accept my belief that morality is an immutable aspect of vision, then it is important to know whether morality can be manifested in more than one way. Let me re-state the question: Does a person's worldview contribute to a private perception of what is moral?

Dr. Fowler's mentor was Lawrence Kohlberg, a psychologist whose life work was centered on the developmental aspects of morality. The great American philosopher, John Dewey, and the Swiss psychologist, Jean Piaget, influenced Kohlberg. Fowler helps us to understand that morality is *not* a yes/no, up/down, black/white state of being. Instead, each of us has an opportunity to move through a developmental series of moral phases. Our individual position relative to these phases helps us to define ourselves and, thereby, our operative level of morality. Our confusion about what is "moral" may be influenced by an unwilling-ness to appreciate this developmental flow. Here is a brief summary of Fowler's developmental phases.

PHASE ONE morality represents the initial level of moral judgment-making. It is a process that is natural to the development of the young child. It's based upon a desire to please and, simultaneously, a desire to avoid punishment. At this level of moral judgment "goodness" and "badness" do not reflect inherent values. Nor are they determined by how one's behavior influences another person. Instead —"good" and "bad" are the result of *immediate* and *tangible* consequences, and the latent desire of the child to receive the warm acknowledgment of parents and other connected adults.

Among adults, Phase One morality is centered upon absolute and unquestioned obedience. At an extreme, it is the morality of Nazi Germany. There is a tendency to see status, wealth and material possessions as the source of power. *But what is important here is that "power " is external to the individul. Since we did not originate and cannot control the antecedents of power, Phase One morality inevitably creates a worldview of scarcity.* Whatever we most want is in short supply and is desired by others. That is why we must be vigilant in guarding what we do have. Regardless of how much or how little we have, we must live in fear that others will take it...or that we don't really deserve it...and that if it is lost, we may not be able to regain it. As a consequence of this reasoning, Phase One morality is fear-driven as well as scarcity-based.

Phase One moral judgments tend to be either/or. There are frequent references to dogma. Gradations of meaning are denied or not seen as meaningful. Situational interpretation and circumstantial explanations are threatening and tend to be dismissed as immoral. Adults whose moral development has stalled at this level are not empathic. Because their locus of control is thoroughly invested in externalized authority, they are not able to receive or validate their own feelings, and so they are affectively flat and unable to acknowledge the feeling of others.

PHASE TWO morality is sometimes described as "the morality of the marketplace". The essence of Phase Two morality is in the question, "What's in it for me?" Another interpretation of Phase Two morality is expressed by the phrase, "success at any price" and the adage that "the means is justified by the end". At this level of morality, being "right" simply means looking out for one's own interests. The idea of "back-scratching" and "horse-trading" is derived from Phase Two morality. An obsessive focus on the "bottom line" is another cultural expression of Phase Two morality.

Decision-making at this level can be highly situational. But the objective is not value-based or mission-driven; the basis of evaluation is elementary selfishness. Transcendent values give way to infantile needs for pleasure-seeking and quick gratification. Rules are important because they help to organize the world and that is, after all, a convenience. But if one is smart enough to break the rules and not get caught, that's OK.

All moral reference points in this phase involve low-level aspects of self-gratification. "I won't steal from you because I don't want you stealing from me." *In Phase Two morality, there is an absence of both transcendent purpose and social responsibility.* The moral creed of Phase Two generally involves some aspect of materialism. There is a bit of Phase Two morality in the Horatio Alger mythology and, of course, it is part of the social creed of industrialism. We see much evidence of Phase Two morality in contemporary politics.

Phase Two decision-making by adults is evidence of arrested moral development. It represents an expression of infantile needs and desires by an adult in an adult environment.

As young children begin to integrate their motor skills and rejoice in their newfound capacity to initiate change in the environment, there is a developmental analog to the Phase Two morality we see in adults. The child demands immediate gratification. There is a high need for pleasure. The child attempts to barter acceptable behavior for rewards. This is an important transitional phase in the child's development of ego and boundary. It is foundational to the child's growing sense of appreciation for self that, in turn, contributes to self-esteem. This transitional phase underlies the child's expanding capacity for autonomy, competence and mastery. When the child is not able to developmentally move forward, the child will often become an adult who then functions at a Phase Two level of moral decision-making.

A wonderfully vivid example of adult Phase Two morality is J. R. Ewing, the hero of the once popular adult soap opera,

Dallas. I believe the popularity of this series can best be explained when we recognize that J. R. Ewing's Phase Two morality is part of our cultural ethos. Ewing's character gave us an opportunity to project our infantile desires in a safe and acceptable way.

PHASE THREE morality emphasizes the importance of group membership; this desire for affinity becomes the primary process for decision-making. Loyalty, dependability and group cohesion are values that, to the Phase Three adult, must be preserved and extended. Morality is seen as doing what is sanctioned by society...following operative rules and custom...and accepting group norms. In his book, *Practical Ethics*, Gordon F. Shea describes this phenomenon by writing: "One maintains loyalty and trust by doing what is expected. One tries to be a *good* neighbor, a *good* citizen, a *good* parent, a *good* business person or whatever is stereotyped as 'good' by one's group or society."

The operative idea is solidarity. Solidarity with the neighborhood, the church, the team, the school, the group, the corporation. "What will the neighbors think?" is not merely an acknowledgment of social pressure; it becomes a moral principle for assessing the correctness of behavior.

In Phase Three, interpersonal morality is not based on reward/punishment (Phase One) or getting something in return (Phase Two). *It is based on a desire to contribute to the happiness of others by maintaining cultural norms.* There is a strong desire for appreciation and approval. Group membership generates warm acceptance and easy affection among those who are willing to march to the group's drum.

There is a sense of community that is highly valued. Fear of the loss of community is one of the ways in which morality is preserved.

For all of these reasons, a desire for conformity suppresses innovation and creativity. Challenging the group directly (confrontation) or indirectly (by making waves) is not accepted. Being a loner is seen as undesirable and even irresponsible. Because of the emphasis on group harmony, there is tendency to deny or avoid problems that are perceived as threatening the integrity of the group. When such problems cannot be avoided, they tend to be met with hostility — sometimes sublimated but often overt.

Phase Three individuals tend to rely on fate, chance and circumstance. Their capacity for accepting individual responsibility is limited by a diffused sense of self There is a reliance on luck. Esoteric meanings are frequently attached to incidental happenings. People at this level seem to have a proclivity for ritualized objects and processes. They tend to carry a rabbit's foot or a lucky coin. They are inclined to never do "X" or always do "Y" prior to an important meeting. They have magical systems for betting on the horses or the lottery or a roulette wheel.

The affinity for group membership often creates situations in which other groups (and members of other groups) are seen as marred or flawed or evil. The force of this logic can lead to the absence of civility, expressions of prejudice and outright hostility. There is often a "group think" mentality associated with Phase Three.

In the development of the child, we see analogs at several places during the child's journey to maturity. Perhaps the most dramatic of these is the sense of peer loyalty and peer identity that is a mark of adolescence. But here, as earlier, these analogs are transitional. In a developmentally supportive environment, they prepare the child for the next phase of the journey.

PHASE FOUR morality is superficially related to Phase Three. But there are two crucial differences. First — one's perspective and affinity is much broader. Rather than identifying with a family or a team or a company, there is an identification with the nation, society or culture. The operative moral principle relates to the effective mainten-ance of social order rather than the molecular representa-tion we saw in Phase Three. This leads to a second crucial difference — a reliance on law and order, and an abiding respect for duly constituted authority.

Altruism becomes an ideal of Phase Four morality. One's responsibilities go beyond self, beyond the molecular group. One's responsibilities should properly seek a national or cultural representation. Transcendent values are comfort-ably a part of Phase Four morality. The good life is an examined life. Through an on-going process of examin-ation, a transformational process occurs. One becomes increasingly values-based and mission-driven.

In their book, *Stages*, Nathaniel Lande and Afton Slade describe Phase Four people in this way: "They are concerned with their society, with doing their duty, obeying the rules, paying their bills on time, fulfilling their taxation obligations, helping their neighbors, accepting service on juries and involving themselves in their communities. They are the strength of the nation."

However, Phase Four people often have difficulty in distinguishing between "law" and "justice". While their vision has been culturally broadened, Phase Four people tend to not have a cosmic perspective or a genuine appreciation for diversity. When Ronald Reagan expressed his belief that somehow God has favored America over all other nations, we witnessed an example of how Phase Four morality can "lock in" one belief system while "locking out" all other belief systems. As a result, Phase Four morality tends to support a dichotomy between "us" and "them". Only the "us" and "them" of Phase Four represent much larger entities than in Phase Three.

PHASE FIVE morality involves an intense desire for independent thinking, an abiding respect for individual beliefs, and a deep commitment to the sanctity of life...all life, everywhere. At this level of morality, membership in a family, group, corporation or nation does not require the automatic acceptance of a prevailing ethos. The social contract acknowledges an individual's intrinsic rights. Phase Five morality literally requires respect for self as well as respect for others. While rules are to be obeyed, they are also open to serious question. Martin Luther King's application of civil disobedience is an example of Phase Five morality at work.

The morality of Phase Five goes beyond the nation; it provides a cosmic perspective that cannot be compressed by geographic boundaries or the application of creeds and dogmas. Phase Five morality acknowledges that ambiguity, uncertainty and chaos are part of the natural order.

Kohlberg has suggested that the Constitution of the United States of America is a Phase Five document that is regularly invoked in defense of Phase Two, Phase Three and Phase Four behaviors. The great Lutheran theologian, Martin Marty, has argued that the blind application of law that confronted Jesus was an example of Phase Three morality to which Christ offered a Phase Five response. Marty, Fowler, M. Scott Peck and others have concluded that many Christians express their religious beliefs through Phase Two or Phase Three or Phase Four morality; and many churches support them in these expressions. But these theologians believe that the Christianity of Christ is a Phase Five moral phenomenon that challenges an individual to achieve an authentic Phase Five perspective of morality.

Let me summarize. Each of these five phases provides a different response to the question, "What is moral behavior?" Each phase establishes distinctive criteria by which the morality of behavior is assessed. And each offers a unique organizing principle to guide a person in the search for the good life. Here are some "trigger" phrases:

PHASE ONE — Reward/punishment/obedience and the desire to please.

PHASE TWO — Marketplace morality: Will it sell? Can I get away with it? Is there an equitable trade-off? Are the benefits commensurate with the risk?

PHASE THREE— Affiliation with and identification through molecular group membership.

PHASE FOUR — Preservation and extension of law and order so as to secure the benefits of peace, safety and opportunity within a meta-community,

PHASE FIVE — An intense search for personal autonomy and meaning within a cosmic order of purpose and service.

These five phases represent a developmental flow. *Our place in this progression is determined by how we see ourselves in relation to others.* There is an exquisite give-and-take between the magnitude of our vision (what is *now* possible) and the magnitude of our faith (what is *ultimately* possible). Growth is not an all-or-nothing process. And so our personal journey may be marked by an uneasy, hesitant exploration as we question old assumptions and learn to accept the consequences of new assumptions.

Notice also that our capacity to fully live by intent requires a Phase Five morality. A poet friend said in a letter to me, "If what I want to express can be said in any other way, then there is no reason to convey the message with a poem. I write a poem when I am out of choices and there is no other way to say what I must express."

Similarly, Phase Five morality is not something to which we aspire. Phase Five morality is an outcome, not an objective. Our vision of what is possible determines when we are able to move toward Phase Five.

The developmental flow of these five phases proceeds from the literal to the symbolic and ultimately to the metaphorical. My friend said that poetry expresses truths than cannot be said any other way. Our progression toward Phase Five is marked by an awareness that while the metaphorical content of a myth may not be literally true, nonetheless myths manifest an enduring truth that cannot otherwise be communicated. For example — Greek and Roman myths express timeless truths. But our realization of these truths does not require us to accept the myths as literally true.

The magnitude of our morality is defined by our vision of what is possible.

When I wrote the above short sentence on paper, suddenly I found myself thinking about the story of Jonah. As a literal truth, it is preposterous to believe that a whale swallowed Jonah whole, and three days later he was returned to shore by way of the whale's burp. Yet there are important and timeless truths in this remarkable story. We are well-advised to consider the metaphorical meaning of Jonah. Here is an interpretation written by Gregg Levoy in his book, *Callings: Finding and Following an Authentic Life*.

> On my bookshelf I have a copy of the pocket-size Jewish Bible issued by the United States Army in World War II. One day, struggling with the ill effects of an unanswered calling of my own, I flipped it open randomly in search of guidance, as I often do with books, and my eye fell directly onto the opening lines of the story of Jonah, that bird in flight, caught between heaven and

earth, between saying "yes" and saying "no". Jonah, fleeing to Tarshish with grim relief, was running to the last place he thought God would ever look for him.

Jonah had been called to preach to the people of Ninevah and refused because he considered himself to be an incompetent preacher. Instead he went to the docks and booked passage on a ship sailing in the opposite direction from Ninevah — to Tarshish. God was neither amused nor fooled. He sent a storm down on the ship, not so much as punishment but as an earnest appeal for a more affirmative response from Jonah. But Jonah, despite being the strongest sailor of them all, the one who knew he could subdue the storm if he chose to take responsibility for his part in creating it, decided instead to avoid dealing with the problem. He went to sleep in the bottom of the boat, a behavior referred to nowadays as denial. Jonah's choice further angered God.

The captain, that spirit of wakefulness, who confronted him with his responsibility for the mounting calamity, roused Jonah. Jonah then proved himself to be a man of considerable courage. He confessed that he was to blame and he offered himself as a sacrifice, telling the frightened crew that throwing him overboard was the only way to make the storm subside. They were decent and disbelieving men, and so they ignored his advice and rowed harder for shore. *By their choice, they became unwitting accomplices to the crime.* When the storm took a violent swipe at the main mast, they changed their minds, tossing Jonah overboard and into the belly of a whale; three days later the whale delivered him to the shores of Ninevah; there he was burped onto the beach without ceremony but a changed man.

The late Abraham Maslow wrote insightfully about Jonah and (so far as I know) was the first to have postulated the "Jonah Complex". Maslow's definition of the Jonah Complex is succinct: *The evasion of one's own growth, setting and accepting low levels of aspiration, the fear of doing what one is capable of doing, voluntary self-crippling, pseudo-stupidity and mock humility.* My first-born, daughter Beth, is a clinical psychologist who practices in New York City. She has a special interest in gifted people who have developed a pattern of self-sabatoge. Although I have not heard her use the phrase, I believe she is referring to what Maslow called the Jonah Complex.

Arthur Koestler wrote (in *The Act of Creation*) that "The guilt of Jonah was that he clung to the trivial and tried to cultivate only his own little garden and his own petty concerns." Koestler is helping us to understand that we cannot cling to the trivial and also create a vision. Levoy tells the story of two clerics who were the first to witness the return of the Messiah. The younger man frantically asked the older priest, "What should we do?" The older priest responded, "Look busy." This small anecdote further illustrates the triviality of Doing in the absence of a prevailing vision.

Levoy's book is about becoming actively authentic, which surely places upon a person the need to answer a call. Since all meaningful work involves transcendent values, answering a call *requires* a vision. The decision to answer a call (or to create a vision) is foundationally a spiritual matter involving inner reality. Our challenge, always, is to be sure that what we do reflects who we are. My Doing must be an extension of my Being; and my Being derives meaning from my vision.

Levoy points out that even Moses, on being called to free the Israelites from Egypt, asked "Who am I to do this thing?" In deciding to be guided by our vision, we may create chaos. *But modern-day physics has demonstrated that chaos is a process of rearrangement out of which a higher order emerges.* In his writing, Deepak Chopra refers often to chaos as "the field of infinite possibilities". This present-day thinker has found new words to express the wisdom of the ancient Greeks. Five centuries before the birth of Christ, Greek creation myths looked upon chaos as "pure potential" from which all things and all beings emerge.

Throughout the book, I've contended that we are spiritual beings with a body, not corporeal beings with a soul. Within the context of this belief I challenge you to consider M. Scott Peck's idea (expressed in *The Road Less Traveled*). He suggests that the endpoint of our lives comes down to "a single terrifying idea, the single most demanding idea in the history of humankind: that God wants us to become Himself (or Herself or Itself). *God is not just the source but the destination of evolution.*"

Peck's words are overwhelming. But the grandeur of Peck's idea gets in the way. That and our own arrogance expressed through our need to complicate what is simple. I love these words by Morton Kelsey, taken from his book, *Companions on the Inner Way*. Kelsey is a Jungian analyst and an Episcopal priest.

We are children. There is no question about Abba receiving us. All we have to do is acknowledge our child-ishness and come. This is the reason why the broken and simple, the poor in spirit, the anxiety-ridden, the mourning, the meek, the unsatisfied and unfulfilled, the hungry and thirsty, the persecuted and ridiculed find it so easy to turn to God. Those who are doing quite well on their own and think they have life securely within their grasp don't like to admit their ultimate helplessness and come as children before Abba.

Shortly before his death and in the same spirit, Carl Jung wrote (in *The Undiscovered Self*) that

I am neither spurred on by excessive optimism nor am I blindly in love with high ideals. I am merely concerned with the fate of the individual human being — that infinitesimal unit on whom a world depends, and, if we read the world's wisdom literature aright, is the primary object of God's concern.

The perspective of these quotations is at the center of a process by which we can find comfort and meaning in a cosmic faith. We can live big and, in gratitude, pray big. We can learn from Jonah.

But our glory is that we need not carry Jonah's fear.

Truth exists; only falsehood has to be invented.

George Braque

Chapter XIII

LIFE, INTELLIGENCE, ENERGY

The paradigm which I described in the ninth chapter raises many interesting and fundamental issues. Here I would like to establish a context to help us better understand whether life energy can be found in simpler forms of life ... and whether this life energy exists after death. I hope to use this information in a way that will assist you to better appreciate your own nature and the nature of the universe, thereby permitting you to function at a higher level of fulfillment and effectiveness.

Item: Molecular biologists are helping us to understand that simple bacteria are able to communicate with each other and that they have a shared sense of community responsibility. If you would like documentation for this amazing statement, permit me to refer you to a lengthy article in the science section of *The New York Times* dated October 13, 1992. The study involved myxobacteria, an evolved form of the comparatively primitive E. coli. Myxobacteria are soil organisms; a single gram of soil may contain up to a million of them. However, they are truly social. For example, in this article Dr. Howard C. Berg of Harvard

University asserts "They forage for food in packs, like wolves, and like wolves they help each other in feeding."

The article explains that these bacteria secrete enzymes to help them consume the carcasses of other bacteria that are lying in the soil. To prevent these enzymes from seeping into the soil, the bacteria are able to signal each other to form a hollow shell which surrounds the food and contains the enzyme. Remarkably, Dr. Dale Kaiser of Stanford University has been able to demonstrate an even greater degree of cooperation by these bacteria during times of scarcity.

When faced with starvation, the bacteria turn into tough spores, which resist freezing and drying, and they are able to survive in a form of suspended animation. These individual spores clump together in groups of about 100,000 in order to create a highly insulated cylinder. These cylinders (called "fruiting bodies") are carried by a passing breeze to more fertile soil.

Dr. Kaiser reports that the communal behavior of these bacteria is distinctly different when they are faced with a scarcity of food or actual starvation, and that they have the "intelligence" to discriminate between these conditions so as to respond appropriately. What occurs is, in fact, a form of communication. Dr. Kaiser has been able to demonstrate a specific "starvation signal" which these bacteria can both send and receive.

The bacteria also have a distinctive signal which is emitted when there are enough of them to form a fruiting body. The signal that this density has been attained is a mixture of eight amino acids. On sensing it, the cells somehow know to come together and form into a pile of cylinders that is "as neatly ordered as logs in a cord of wood". Each cell in the array is responsible for producing a specific protein that signals its neighbor to "turn on" a special set of genes. It is under the influence of these genes that the bacteria lose their usual configuration and become round so that a cylinder can be formed.

Item: Dr. James Shapiro, a molecular biologist at the University of Chicago, has been studying the ways in which various bacteria are able to create highly elaborate and *purposefully* disciplined geometric constructs ... and how these constructs (or community organizations) change according to environmental conditions. He has shown that when the social configuration changes, apparently on cue, the individual bacteria somehow know to behave differently.

For example — when the bacteria are in a milieu that is rich in food, the community creates an intricate "pinwheel" and each member of the community rotates in a way that directs nutrients into the center of the community. But when a mildly toxic substance is introduced into the milieu, hundreds of thousands of bacteria immediately create a closed geometric form and, in an apparently coordinated and disciplined manner, they begin to rotate in a way which directs the toxin away from the center of the community. [The previously cited article in *The New York Times* also describes Shapiro's work.]

Item: A report was published in the February 1, 1992 *Proceedings of the National Academy of Science* which described the work of two botanists, Bruce E. Mahall, and Regan M. Calloway, University of California at Santa Barbara. Apparently at least some plants communicate directly with each other through their root systems; amazingly, these communications seem to involve both a sense of community and what might be termed "intelligence".

The process under study is technically known as "allelopathy" — a phenomenon which allows plants of different species to achieve ecological equilibrium by stimulating and/or inhibiting neighboring plants via chemicals which are exuded from their roots. The nature of the chemical message changes in response to the subterranean ecology. In other words, when the ecological circumstances change, so also does the chemical message.

These botanists are suggesting there is strong experimental evidence this communication involves more than chemical stimulation-and-response. There seems to be a form of "intelligence" by which these root systems are making "judgments" and then situationally invoking a response that is unique to a particular circumstance. The investigators also explore the possibility that plants may be able to distinguish between "self" and "non-self" in a process that is somewhat parallel to the way in which animal immune systems recognize foreign substances.

Item: I think you will be intrigued by a discovery reported in *The New York Times* on November 17, 1992. Let me quote directly from the article.

Plants, unlike animals, have no nerves, so scientists have been jolted by the discovery this month that the ordinary tomato plant uses an electric signal to alert its defense system against grazing caterpillars. A team of researchers from England and New Zealand reported in the November 5 issue of *Nature* that when a leaf on a tomato seedling is chewed by insects, it sends out electrical warning signals, alerting the rest of the plant to the danger. As undamaged leaves receive the electric signal, they begin producing defensive chemicals that make the leaves difficult to digest.

"It's a very exciting result," said Dr. Keith Roberts, head of the cell biology department at the John Innis Institute in England and the author of the commentary that was published with the article. "It's really a conceptual breakthrough to realize that plants use electrical signals in the same way animals use them in nerve cells. It brings plants a little bit closer to animals." Dr. David Wildon, a plant physiologist at the University of East Anglia, England, and one of the authors of the new study, said: *"Everyone can now see that if you find a system in animals and you look for it in plants, it turns up. The more we look, the more similarities there are."* [Emphasis added]

Item: In Dr. Larry Dossey's notable book, *Recovering the Soul,* he shares some statistically elegant experiments, including double-blind crossover studies, in which large trays of rye seeds were divided into side A and side B. Both sides received identical environmental stimuli: Temperature, sun, soil nutrients, water, etc.

But volunteers "prayed" for seed on one of the two sides. I put the word "pray" in quotation because some volunteers, by their choice, did not "pray" but instead sent "positive energy". At a given time, the shoots were harvested, washed and dried. The prayed-for seeds were consistently statistically more productive.

As an elaboration of this experiment, investigators decided to stress the seeds by introducing saline into the water. Again the prayed-for seeds did better, and by a greater margin. The more stressed the seeds, the greater was the measurable effects of the prayer/positive energy.

Item: Cardiologist Randolph Byrd, formerly a professor at the University of California School of Medicine, designed an experiment which has been reported in the medical literature. During a ten-month study, a computer randomly assigned 393 patients in the coronary care unit at San Francisco General Hospital either to a sampling which was prayed for by prayer groups throughout the nation (192 patients) or to a group that was not supported in prayer (201 patients).

According to Dossey, "The study was designed according to the most rigid criteria that can be used in clinical studies, meaning that it was a randomized, prospective, double-blind experiment in which neither the patients, nurses nor doctors knew which group the patients were in." Those who were participating in the prayer groups knew the first name of the patient and had a very brief statement of their condition. Each of the prayer volunteers prayed for many different patients. But each patient in the experiment had between five and seven people praying for him or her. Dossey summarized the study with these remarkable conclusions:

Prayed-for patients were five times less likely than the control group to require antibiotics. They were three times less likely to develop pulmonary edema. None of the prayed-for group required endotracheal intubation (compared with twelve in the unremembered group who required mechanical ventilation support). Fewer patients in this group died.

Here are some words from Dossey's book: "*If the technique being studied had been a new drug or surgical procedure instead of prayer, it would almost certainly have been heralded as some sort of 'breakthrough'*. Even hard boiled skeptics seem to agree on the significance of Byrd's findings. Dr. William Nolan, a physician who has written a book debunking faith healing, acknowledged that 'apparently this study will stand up to scrutiny. Maybe we doctors ought to be writing on our work sheets, *Pray three times a day*. If it works, it works.'"

Dossey then continues: "This rigorous study suggests that something about the mind allows it to intervene in the course of distant happenings, such as the clinical course of patients in a coronary care unit hundreds of thousands of miles away. In this study, the degree of spatial separation did not seem to matter. Byrd discovered that prayer groups just around the corner from the hospital were no more effective than those hundreds of miles away."

Dossey points out that apparently some form of energy is involved. It must be a special form of energy since the intensity of it does not decrease with distance.

I am not arguing in support of the power of God. Of course, I have my own views and I am happy to share them. But my opinions and beliefs are extraneous to this discussion. Here I am simply suggesting that there is some form of what appears to be energy that ordinary people can purposefully direct. The definition and exercise of this energy can be within the traditions and nomenclature of organized religion. But as measured by effectiveness, and as documented in Byrd's study, apparently this isn't necessary.

Item: Physicists tell us that 97-98% of an atom is empty space. Of course, atoms comprise molecules. Each of us is a collection of molecules...and so it logically follows that each of us is composed of 97-98% empty space. Curiously, when a person is cremated, the non-combustible remains weigh about two to three percent of the living weight.

Your automobile is also mostly empty space. But if you drive your automobile into a telephone pole, which, too, is mostly empty space, you may sustain serious injury. That's because you were not driving at the square of the speed of light. Were you to attain this speed, Einstein's famous formula tells us that you would not be injured.

Most of you have seen *Star Trek* in its original or many derivative forms. "Beam me up, Scotty," is an apparently fanciful demonstration of "matter transport" which, according to quantum physics, is entirely plausible.

Consider now the significance of the concept that all of us, on the molecular level, are mostly energy. This insight alone gives us reason to redefine what we mean by "disease" and, of course, what we mean by "health" and "wellness". We must also redefine how we become sick and how we get better. (Is "disease" a condition which effects the 3% of us that has substance or the 97% of us that doesn't?)

As we begin to realize that more than 97% of each of us is formless and insubstantial, we have an opportunity to reconsider some of our most basic assumptions. For example:

Item: Let me briefly return to a subject already discussed. But in this context, I would like to again bring it to your attention. Where in your mostly empty body will we find what is commonly termed your "mind"? Is your mind between your ears? Is it a function of your brain? An electrical function? A biochemical function?

There is now considerable evidence that your mind represents what philosophers call a "non-local event". Your brain may be a trans-receiver which has the ability to connect with various aspects of what might be termed a "super-mind" and that, potentially, you are able to draw upon and even retrieve the knowledge and experiences of every person who has ever lived.

While this seems to be an outrageous insult to common sense, let me remind you that Jung and others have found common patterns, symbols, stories and myths among all people — regardless of locale or age. Probably you know that Dr. Jung postulated the existence of a "collective unconscious" to explain these phenomena.

Consider again, Rupert Sheldrake's hypothesis. He proposes that the form, development and behavior of living organisms are shaped and maintained by specific energy fields as yet unrecognized by any science. *These fields are in some manner determined by the form and behavior of past organisms of the same species through direct connections which cross both space and time.* If his hypothesis is correct, we must significantly modify the work of Darwin. Dr. Sheldrake is arguing that the knowledge and experiences of past generations actually change the performance potential of future generations through alterations in these energy fields.

Before you close your mind to the possibility I'm here suggesting, I urge you to read Dossey's *Recovering the Soul.* And if you are curious, the bibliography that's part of his book will provide an excellent point of entry for your own research.

Item: About 30 years ago, Russian scientists reported the development of a photographic technique for recording the energy auras that were emitted by Egyptian mummies. These auras, technically known as Kirlian auras, seemed to be a unique energy field that is associated with every living thing; and that after death, the aura continues, even for 3,000 years. A *National Geographic* team was able to replicate the work of the Russians and today the recording of Kirlian auras is old hat. The existence of them, however, does seem to require an alteration in how we define "life" and "death" just as we must also revise the classic definition that separated plants from animals.

Item: Physicists tell us that energy can be transformed but not destroyed. Each of the mostly empty atoms in my body contain energy. Is it possible that these atoms create in perpetuity an energy field that is a unique representation of me? Is it possible for me to somehow project my energy in support of your well-being — regardless of whether my hands are touching you or you are on the other side of the planet? Is it possible that after my death, the information encoded in my unique energy field becomes part of a vast reservoir of energy which you can learn to draw upon and apply? Is it possible that this energy — regardless of whether we refer to it as Jehovah or God or White Light or Abbyjabby — is a spiritual gift? Is it possible that all of us are, in fact, spiritual creatures with a body rather than animal creatures with a spirit?

It would appear that a comprehensive definition of life is not easily reached. That willful intelligence may be exercised by bacteria and plants. And that a unique presentation of energy may continue for thousands of years beyond what traditionally we've known as death. Clearly — our definitions and our perspectives are not congruent with our knowledge. And so we must seek new ways to create wholeness.

To confront a person with his own attitudes is to show him his own light.

Carl Jung

Chapter XIV

INNER ATTITUDES, OUTER LIVES

Some questions to ponder: Is it possible that our inner thoughts have the power to change the outer reality of our world? Can the energy of our thoughts be summoned by choice? And directed by intent?

Perhaps these questions seem a bit unworldly to a group of men and women who accommodate and respond to specific realities in what is commonly seen as the real world. I dare to ask these questions because there is a growing body of scientific evidence which demonstrates that each of us has inner resources which far exceed our cultural expectations. What we are learning is that the power of our inner mind is not a myth woven by poets from gossamer threads. The power of our inner mind is a hard scientific truth.

This is not a new idea, of course. The roots of this idea can be seen clearly in the wisdom literature of the world. More recently, most of you are familiar with James L. Allen's powerful little book, *As a Man Thinketh*. The thrust of Allen's argument is that each of us, by the thoughts we generate, is empowered to create our own reality. The great

American philosopher, William James, offered the same message in this emphatic and concise sentence: *"By changing the inner attitudes of their minds, human beings can change the outer aspects of their lives."* Most of us are comfortable accepting this argument, non-specifically and poetically. But now I am asking you to consider the possibility that the argument is cognitively valid and with specific, worldly applications.

Item: In a carefully controlled scientific experiment, a reputable scientist, Marilyn J. Schlitz, PhD, placed a number of subjects in their own private rooms. Each subject could be seen via closed-circuit TV, and each subject was also attached to sophisticated monitoring equipment which measured autonomic (involuntary) physiological responses.

Observers, who were physically separated from the subjects, were asked to stare intently at the video image of a randomly chosen and unaware subject. At a frequency that far exceeded statistical probability, the stared-at subjects showed physiological evidence of stress, as measured by changes in skin temperature, respiratory and pulse rates and galvanic skin response.

Item: Because a colleague of the reporting scientist, Richard Wiseman, PhD, was skeptical of these published results, he attempted to replicate them using the same protocol and methodology. But he found no evidence that staring at the video image of a subject influenced the subject's physiology. His results were entirely consistent with the laws of scientific probability.

Item: The inconsistency of their results intrigued both scientists and so they decided to work together. They used the same physical facility and drew from the same group of subjects and observers. The same equipment was used, always consistent with the established methodology. Moreover, each scientist monitored the work of the other to assure conformance with the protocol. Remarkably, the first scientist was able to conclusively confirm her initial result, that staring at the video image of the subject would influence the subject's physiology. But here's the intriguing aspect of this situation. Dr. Wiseman was also able to confirm his initial finding, that the laws of statistics adequately explained the observations which he had collected.

Let me quote from a report prepared by the first scientist, Dr. Marilyn J. Schlitz: *"Under these circumstances, where all other factors were controlled, it appears that the only explanation for the difference in the two sets of data has to do with the intentions and expectations of the experimenters.... These results [would seem to] support the hypothesis that conscious energy can interact directly with the physical world, that experimenters cannot be seen as detached from the object of their studies, and that beliefs and expectations make a difference, even under conditions in which the results cannot be explained by ordinary sensory interactions."*

Please take a moment and contemplate the implications of the above italicized quotation. If this observation by Dr. Schlitz is valid, then we must revise significantly our understanding of "objectivity" and the scientific method. Dr. Schlitz is suggesting the possibility of a "new" science in which there is not a valid separation of the observer from the observed.

Each, apparently, is a manifestation of the other and each influences the other. Let me point out that this perspective seems to be entirely consistent with what contemporary physicists tell us about the behavior of sub-atomic particles: When a particle is observed, its behavior is altered. Of course, Dr. Schlitz is dealing with that magnificently elegant organization of sub-atomic particles which we know as the human creature. It would seem that the same principles which are relevant on a sub-atomic level may also explain how we influence each other.

In this experiment, subjects were physically separated from the observers but were within the same building. Suppose the subjects were in a building across the street? A hundred miles away? Five thousand miles away? Would the results have been different? And is it necessary for an observer to stare at a video image? Might the observer hold a photograph and stare at it? Or more provocatively, what would happen if an observer merely focused intently on a mental image of the subject?

These questions are true paradigm-busters. Whether you are a brain surgeon, operate a gravel pit or sell life insurance, I believe that how you consider these questions will directly influence the quality of your life. As a futurist, let me offer a slam-dunk prognostication: *Over the next ten years, the methodical investigation of directed energy, mental and spiritual, will be one of the great meta-themes of the life sciences.* Already there are at least a half dozen schools of medicine where on both undergraduate and graduate levels students are being introduced to various expressions of the fundamental life force that I am here calling directed energy.

There is at least one principle of contemporary physics, which as far as I know, is still unchallenged: Energy can be transformed but not destroyed. And so it's useful to consider what in the literature is referred to as Kirlian energy. More than 30 years ago, Russian scientists were able to demonstrate that 2,500-year-old mummies emitted a characteristic energy which could be recorded on a photographic plate. There are now many demonstrations of this energy, known as Kirlian auras, in the literature. This suggests that "death", which we have always regarded as an absolute, is not totally dissimilar to "life" since energy is an aspect of both states of being.

Earlier I noted that each atom in our bodies is about 97% empty space. I also offered that the weight of non-combustible remains of a cremated body are about 3% of the live weight. And so ultimately we must ask ourselves some very difficult questions. At death, what happens to the energy that was in our bodies? Where does it go? Is it transformed? Into what? Let me suggest that our inner attitudes toward these questions has something to do with the outer reality we create for ourselves.

As we come to realize that apparently opposite qualities of being may be different manifestations of the same phenomenon, our traditional categories seem to merge. Integration displaces separation. For example: When a caterpillar is chewing on a leaf of the common tomato plant, the leaf biochemically communicates its distress to the roots. The roots respond by introducing a bitter substance into the sap that is distasteful to caterpillars. Conceptually this is not too different from the biochemical communication we experience as we respond to perceived danger. The harder we look at plants, the more they resemble animals. And so we are bridging the previously absolute separation between botany and zoology.

But there's more. Let's now consider another way in which inner reality influences outer reality. Scientists are beginning to learn about the study of pheromones. We now know that at least some attitudes and behaviors are associated with the generation of a characteristic odor that cannot be perceived consciously. For this reason, some writers have referred to pheromones as "olfactory hormones". Of course, scent is an important part of our life experiences. A re-experienced bouquet of a favored food from a long-ago meal is powerful! The use of perfumes to augment the natural odors of the body is related to both sensuality and sexuality, and has a history of at least 5,000 years. But now we are coming to understand that odors *which we cannot consciously perceive* still have emphatic physiologic consequences.

For unnumbered generations many women have accepted the folk wisdom that when there is prolonged association with other women, as in a family circle, college dormitory or prison, individual menstrual cycles become synchronous. In 1992 this was scientifically demonstrated to be valid and, moreover, the reason relates to the sub-clinical olfactory perception of certain pheromones that are associated with menstruation.

If you will think about it for a moment, this is a pretty important discovery because it's telling us that an odor which cannot be consciously detected is nonetheless sufficiently powerful to cause hormonal change. We now know that there are characteristic pheromones generated by specific attitudes. Many of these have been identified. We can define chemically the pheromone that is associated with fear; and it has been shown that many animals, including canines and humans, are able to detect this odor. Anger generates a characteristic pheromone. So also does pessimism ... and, happily, optimism. And there is a known pheromone that is associated with feelings of well-being and tranquility.

We are now able to say with scientific assurance that each of us, by reason of our attitudes, is directly responsible for either enriching or polluting our immediate environment ... the same environment which contains our colleagues, our clients and our families.

Let me again offer you the words of William James: "By changing the inner attitudes of their minds, human beings can change the outer aspects of their lives." Today we have considerable knowledge about how an individual can take to heart what William James has said and accept responsibility for oneself. Let me ask you to consider several not-too-imaginary situations in the hope that you will readily relate to one of them. Imagine yourself sitting alone on a beach, lost in your own thoughts as you watch the sun's setting. Or taking a quiet morning walk along the beach. A peaceful hike in the forest. Think about staring into a campfire. Resting easily in a summer meadow. Or perhaps listening to a favorite piece of music.

These pristine experiences give us a sense of centeredness and well-being. We feel tranquil and in our tranquility we have a sense of wholeness and, thereby, personal power. At least for these moments, all things seem possible.

There is another extremely important aspect to these experiences: They are timeless. When we are in the middle of these experiences, we don't have a sense of time. We are engulfed by the experience. But we do not perceive the experience as having a beginning … middle … or end. The experience simply *is*. And, remarkably, it is simple. These timeless experiences are a basic aspect of the human condition. They are nurturing. They are healing. They are restorative.

During these experiences, our brain slows and a characteristic brain wave (which we identify as alpha) triggers an important biochemical response. Our vascular system becomes more elastic, causing blood pressure to lessen. Capillary flow is enhanced and so our skin is warmer. Heart, pulse and respiration are slowed. Our immune system is strengthened by an increase in the number and motility of T-cells. The slowing of our brain waves also suppresses activity in the glands which otherwise would prepare us for "fight or flight". As a result, our bodies do not receive the hormones associated with stress. That's one of the reasons why the enzymes excreted by our skin are different during these alpha periods.

We now understand that during these alpha periods, we are best able to grasp new patterns of being. We become more holistic in our outlook. We are better integrated in that we have more ready access to our best hopes and highest aspirations. We are better able to see new ways ... new combinations as the conscious and subconscious aspects of our mind are integrated.

By way of comparison, virtually all of us spend most of our waking day dealing with the identification and resolution of problems and/or opportunities. In this circumstance, the brain waves generated by our brain are characteristically known as beta waves. The primary characteristic of beta waves relates to the number of cycles per second at which they are occurring — significantly more than when we are in our alpha state. It's interesting to note that infants spend most of the day in alpha. A child's capacity for beta tends to increase as we begin to ask the child to accept adult-like responsibilities. Generally by the time of first grade, most children are already spending a third to a half of their waking hours in beta. But it is important to realize that the fantasies and imaginary play of children continues to enrich these beta experiences.

It's not that beta is somehow bad or dangerous or wrong. Not at all! Beta provides us with the physiological responses that are appropriate to the essential activities of defining and resolving problems and opportunities. But without the enrichment of our inner life through the exercise of our potential for alpha, we tend to experience more stress and fatigue … have less access to the power and beauty of our own being … and we become less effective in all of our life activities.

Nearly 30 years ago I had the extreme good fortune of learning about how I could use biofeedback to benefit my well-being. At the time this experience was offered to me, it was a palliative for an intractable medical condition. But now I realize that my experiences with biofeedback were a gift of incalculable value because with biofeedback I am almost always able to quickly put myself into an alpha state, anywhere, any time. Most of my working life, I am in the service of my clients. It is fatiguing to be an active, connected listener over a prolonged period, often interspersed with travel and, sometimes, too much entertainment. But even today, after 30 years' of experience, I marvel at how renewed I feel when I am able to give myself the privilege of choosing 15 minutes of biofeedback rather than lunch.

Whether for you it is Bach, biofeedback or a walk on the beach isn't the issue. The issue is helping you to help yourself get in touch with the vitality and validity of your inner reality — your most prized and deeply cherished attitudes, beliefs and values. I believe this is a crucial personal responsibility for each of us. Until we accept and act upon this responsibility, we are stuck in the probabilities of our lives while the possibilities of our lives are always seeming to be out of reach.

My message is simple. First, each of us has within ourself access to enormously powerful emotional and spiritual resources. Second, we can learn to direct these forces by our own volition. Third, as we gain the skill to direct them, these inner resources have the power to change the outer realities of our lives. Fourth, there is a rapidly expanding body of science which helps us to appreciate that our inner power and its consequences are real and discernible. Fifth, when we permit ourselves to be renewed through alpha-generating activities, we amplify the force of our inner resources and our capacity to direct them.

As we come to appreciate the creative power of the past in helping us to envision a future of choice, we begin to move beyond the restrictions of probabilities and toward the splendor of possibilities.

Ralph Waldo Emerson wrote that "What lies behind us and what lies before us are tiny matters compared to what lies within us." The possibility that he is precisely correct gives each of us an opportunity that cannot be weighed…and certainly cannot be denied. Regardless of your task responsibilities, suppose you came to believe passionately in Emerson's words. What would that mean to your career? Or to your family responsibilities? Would it influence your community contributions? How?

Earlier I told you about watching my then six-year-old daughter, Martha, learn some flowing gymnastic movements on a balance beam that had been placed on the floor of the gym. The story is again pertinent. Each week the beam was raised six inches. How remarkable it was to watch each child's self-perception change as the beam was raised!

At even a few inches above the floor, the gymnastic movements of most kids were clearly cramped and over-controlled compared to when the beam was on the floor. I wonder if this isn't an apt metaphor for how so many of us react to a new adventure. Until we are able to passionately believe in Emerson's words and the realness of our own inner reality, we are stuck in the morass of life's probabilities. But if we were to believe passionately in Emerson's words and, as a result, in every aspect of our lives we found new opportunities for joy-filled service, how would our individual sense of self be changed?

When we permit these questions to reside only in the outer realities of our lives, the questions are intellectualized as hypothetical constructs. The questions are quite literally outside of ourselves; they become remote and separate. But when we absorb these questions and intensely commit ourselves to act upon them, they are not remote. They become the behavioral equivalent of nuclear energy. Perhaps the most marvelous gift of all is that this power is immediately available to each of us. Now! Not someday. We need no one's permission. There is no tuition or entrance examination or necessary equipment. And no prerequisites.

In a cultural *tour de force*, Nike introduced the slogan, "Just do it." That is my best wish for you.

A cheerful heart is good medicine, but
a downcast spirit dries up the bones.

Proverbs 17:22

Chapter XV

MAY THE FORCE BE WITH YOU!

A continuing theme of my work is that through an alteration of inner attitudes, we are empowered to change our outer reality. An interesting application of this theme involves what we are learning about longevity. It used to be said that if you want to live to be 100, you must carefully pick your grandparents. While genetics *is* a factor, we now know that in most circumstances, it is a minor factor. Diet and exercise are certainly important. But there is now considerable evidence in the literature that these are secondary factors. *We are learning that an individual's attitudes — indeed, certain specific attitudes — seem to be the primary determinants of longevity.*

The literature of behavioral medicine now provides more than 300 studies (many are statistically quite elegant) which predictably link attitude to physiological outcome. For example — among a group of 3,000 adults who presented without evidence of frank disease, the best predictor of whether each person would confront a life-threatening illness during the subsequent ten years was the person's response to three core issues:

First — how a person *feels* about his/her work. **Second** — how a person *feels* about his/her relationships. **Third** — how a person *feels* about his/her health. These three attitudinal clusters were more predictive than any combination of laboratory tests and physician examination. (Not so incidentally, nearly two-thirds of people who suffer a heart attack prior to age 50 did not have any significant physical risk factors.)

I have enormous respect for Larry Dossey, a physician who is board-certified in internal medicine and also holds an earned PhD in psychology. In his book, *Meaning and Medicine*, he tells us:

> The best study of the impact of people's opinions on their health involved more than 2,800 men and women age 65 and over. It was conducted by sociologist Ellen Idler of Rutgers University and Stanislav Kasl of the Department of Epidemiology and Public Health at Yale Medical School. Their findings are consistent with results from five other large studies involving more than 23,000 people, age 19 to 94. All of these studies bring us to the same conclusion: Our own opinion about the state of our health is a better predictor than such objective factors as physical symptoms, findings from exams and laboratory tests or behaviors such as cigarette smoking.

About six years ago, a group of medical researchers intensely studied nearly 5,000 men and women who had reached or surpassed the age of 100. *There were no significant patterns in diet, exercise or family history.* But there were five sets of attitudes which these centenarians often seemed to share.

First of all, throughout their adult life there was repeated evidence of what the investigators called "passion". It might have been singing in a church choir ... gardening ... volunteer work ... restoring antique furniture or cars ... or whatever. The activity was not important. But the individual's passionate commitment to the activity was! In many of the centenarian's lives, the activity would change from time to time. But not the *quality* of the passionate commitment.

The second meaningful set of attitudes involved what the investigators called "purpose". These people persisted in finding meaningful channels of service to others. They saw themselves as values-based and mission-driven. They wanted to be a contributing member of a community. A sense of affiliation with the community was important to them. They wanted to feel "belonged".

The third factor was an extraordinary resiliency in the lives of these people, especially with regard to personal tragedies. They were able to find deep and abiding meaning in their personal losses and so their losses, while not forgotten or ignored, were integrated into their ongoing lives.

Fourth, these men and women were regularly physically active. Perhaps as part of an organized or structured exercise program. But not necessarily. What they shared was an active involvement in caring for themselves. They wanted mobility. They accepted physical limitations. But they found ways, physically and attitudinally to feel free — regardless of their circumstance.

Finally, there was a significant pattern of curiosity which was evident throughout the lives of these centenarians. Many of them had limited formal education. Not all of them enjoyed reading. But in the words of one investigator, "They sure liked to ask 'why' a lot." Other words which the investigators used to describe this group were "openness" and "wonderment".

Clearly, then, there is considerable reason for believing that attitude is a primary determinant of longevity. *Notice, please, that the factors cited above are concerned with qualities of life, not quantities of life.* These factors seem to relate to an individual's capacity for fun and fulfillment. From my perspective, longevity apparently relates to an individual's willingness to make personally optimal choices, e.g., to live by intent.

Living by intent is a *natural* life strategy. To have fun while seeking fulfillment produces a *quality* of life that, in turn, has the potential for generating *quantities* of life benefits. The literature provides us with many studies of the classic Type A personality. These studies suggest that to *not* have fun and to displace fulfillment with maintenance may seriously impede both the quality and quantity of life. *Dollars follow attitudes. . . not the other way around.* When an emphasis on dollars comes first, evidently there is a raised probability that life will be diminished — qualitatively and in abbreviated tenure.

Permit me to suggest that functionally the opposite of "fun" and "fulfillment" is "helplessness" and "hopelessness". The literature of behavioral medicine amply demonstrates that prolonged feelings of helplessness and hopelessness are especially significant in predicting the likelihood of life-threatening disease or accident. I'm reminded of a famous and often-repeated experiment which took place at the University of Pennsylvania in the early 1960s under the direction of Dr. Martin Seligman, a psychologist.

Laboratory animals were placed within a checkerboard of wire cages and brief, low-level electric shocks were randomly and intermittently delivered to the feet of the animals. When the enclosures were constructed in a way that permitted the animals to jump over a barrier in order to reach a cage that was temporarily shock-free, they were able to tolerate repeated shocks without seriously compromising their physiology.

But when the enclosures had high walls and animals were confined to a single cage which was intermittently shocked, after a while the animals seemed to passively accept the trauma. In human terms, the animals experienced a chronic sense of helplessness and hopelessness. Coincident with their learned helplessness and hopelessness, the animals developed a characteristic and striking disease profile which included gastrointestinal ulceration, auto-immune disorders and malignant tumors.

The literature now provides compelling statistical evidence that when helplessness and hopelessness are learned by children in their early lives, there is an enhanced probability of certain adult disease profiles including some forms of cancer, rheumatoid arthritis and lupus.

I hope that the very important work of Dr. Candace Pert will someday allow her to be recognized as a Nobel Laureate. When she was director of the brain chemistry section of the National Institutes of Health, Dr. Pert was able to demonstrate that neuropeptides are manufactured throughout the body, not just in the brain, *and that it is appropriate to regard each cell as having a latent intelligence within itself.*

The idea that every cell in our body has what might be termed "intelligence" is breath-taking and full of implications. It means that as an organism, we have a virtually unlimited capacity for accommodation and response to the dysfunctions which appear as disease. *On a cellular level, the body has an innate capacity to heal.*

Let me offer a model which may clarify what I've been discussing. Here is my sense of a progressive flow which influences all of us.

1. Our current perceptions *and* our prior experiences *and* our expectations for the future create a constellation of attitudes which, consciously and unconsciously, cause physiologic response. *Attitudes drive our thoughts, which drive our physiology.* What's in me surrounds me.

2. We then place meaning (which is expressed through feelings) on these responses. For example — when we expect the worst, we increase the possibility of it happening.

3. These meanings (feelings) contribute to the probability of repeating the cycle; and with each repetition, the cycle is reinforced.

4. We are able to alter this process by modifying our perceptions and/or reinterpreting our experiences and/or recasting our expectations.

5. Over a period of time, this provides us with an opportunity for making new choices which, in turn, have the potential for creating new attitudes.

6. In this way, we are able to generate a different, more positive and choice-driven set of physiological responses.

7. These different physiological responses support us in attaching new meanings to the responses.

8. Through this alteration of meaning, our feelings change.

9. And so here we have the potential for positive reinforcement.

10. Through these associated processes, we are able to change our outer reality. Here is another way of saying this: By these processes we are able to organize our outer reality so that it authentically reflects our inner reality.

HERE'S WHAT I BELIEVE: *Neither our attitudes nor our physiology are pre-ordained. Our biology is not our destiny. All of us have an enormous capacity for choice (what I refer to as "living by intent"). This capacity is largely unrecognized, unacknowledged and, therefore, unappreciated. But it exists. And it reaches far beyond the limited ways most of us have been taught to respond to our circumstances.*

The power of one's expectations — spoken and unspoken, conscious and unconscious — cannot be overestimated. Let me describe for you an experiment which took place in the early 1970s. (Consider the implications of this experiment to parenting, teaching or our penal system.)

Investigators rang a bell immediately before injecting laboratory rats with a drug that suppressed T cell production in the bone marrow of subject animals. This process was repeated for several days — bell-ringing followed by drug injection. Then the investigators substituted an inert substance for the active drug, but otherwise maintained the protocol of the experiment. *Even with placebo, the animals still realized a depressed immune response.* Somehow the "intelligence" within the cells of subject animals was able to create a physiological response in the absence of a direct stimulus. Attitude determined physiology.

But there is more to say. After several days of bell-ringing and injection, investigators merely rang a bell and did not inject the subject rats. Nonetheless their T cell production was depressed. I repeat: The power of one's expectations — spoken and unspoken, conscious and unconscious — cannot be overestimated. *Expectation influences attitude, even on the level of the cell, and this, in turn, influences behavior, again on the cellular level.*

From the perspective of quantum physics, what I am calling "expectation" is, in fact, a field of energy. Expectations cannot be understood as merely a psychological phenomenon; they are also an energetic phenomenon. We also now know that even in the absence of expectation, the energy field still exists and can be drawn upon by those who seek it. That is the basis for what over the past 25 years has come to be known as "therapeutic touch". I acknowledge that there is an aura of child-like magic to what I am now telling you. But I would like you to know that if you chose to spend a couple of hours in a good research library, you would be able to find considerable hard data in support of what I am describing. For the moment, let me quote some paragraphs from Dr. Larry Dossey's book, *Meaning and Medicine*.

> To evaluate whether or not healing can take place when hands are held a short distance from the body but without physical contact, and without the patient being aware of any healing intent, researcher Daniel P. Wirth performed a double-blind study involving 44 patients with artificially created, full-skin-thickness surgical wounds. The subjects would, for five minutes at a time, insert their arm with the wound through a circular hole cut out in a wall beyond which they could not see. They were falsely told that the purpose of this procedure was to measure "biopotentials" from the surgical wound site with a non-contact device. A non-contact therapeutic touch practitioner was present in the adjoining room only during sessions for the 23 patients of the active treatment group; the room was vacant during the sessions for the remaining 21 patients. As the practitioner attempted to heal the wounds, she meticulously avoided any physical contact with the subjects. At several stages, each wound was measured for healing by a physician who was unaware of the group to which each patient belonged.

> Importantly, since the subjects had no idea they were participating in an experiment of wound-healing, they did not believe they were receiving a healing treatment,

and since they received neither overt nor covert suggestions of being participants in a healing experiment, the placebo response, suggestion, expectation or belief cannot be held responsible for the healing that occurred.

The results were highly significant statistically in many ways. By the eighth day, the wound sizes of the treated subjects showed much less variation than those of the untreated subjects and were significantly smaller. This was also true on the 16th day, when in addition, 13 of the 23 treated subjects were completely healed (wound size zero), compared with none of the untreated group. This study indicated that non-contact therapeutic touch is an effective method of healing wounds, even if the subject is unaware of its occurrence.

Based on the best current literature, the fact is that any of us have the potential for learning to enhance our innate healing power; through this power, we can help others. *And we can also help ourselves*. The study referred to by Dr. Dossey does not stand alone. There are more than one hundred in the literature, and many of them are quite well designed.

Here, then, is provocative evidence of how our inner attitudes can influence our outer reality. There is much more to say about energy, particularly if we concern ourselves with the source of energy.

From time to time, I've used the words *local* and *non-local*. The distinction is straightforward. *Local* phenomena represent a manifestation of cause and event. They occur within our expectation (scientific and cultural) of the time-space continuum. *Local* phenomena meet the test of common sense and observability. By contrast, *non-local* phenomena break all the rules — including those of the time-space continuum. *Non-local* phenomena are counter-intuitive and, indeed, might even be described as zany. They represent a shattering of mental models. Not a tweaking. Not a modification. "Shattering" is exactly the right word.

Classically, physicists have postulated the existence of four physical forces: gravity, electromagnetism and what are referred to as "strong" and "weak" nuclear forces. From the perspective of classical (pre-quantum but post-Einstein) physics, these four forces are eternal. They have been present for all time and they will be present for all time. They were established at the moment of the birth of the universe — the Big Bang. From time to time physicists have speculated about other forces. But only these four forces have been scientifically demonstrated. These forces are intrinsic to all *local* phenomena.

Over the past 30 years, quantum physicists have described *non-local* phenomena as having three unique character-istics which separate them from *local* phenomena. The first of these characteristics is known in the quantum literature as **unmediated** which means that the *non-local* event is not propagated by any type of force, energy or signal. The second characteristic is **unmitigated** which means that the strength of the *non-local* event does not weaken with increasing distance or, conversely, strengthen as distance is reduced. Whether at an inch or a million miles, a *non-local* event displays the same vigor. Finally, the third force is **immediate.** This simply means that a *non-local* event does not have a separate cause. Cause *and* event simultaneously exist. There is total spontaneity or, to say it another way, there is not timeline between any two or more aspects of a *non-local* event.

If you permit yourself to creatively wander from quantum physics to theology, sociology, psychotherapy, philosophy, political science . . . indeed, any organized discipline . . . it quickly becomes clear that quantum physics provokes implications that are much more metaphysical than physical. If two previously connected subatomic particles are separated and any behavior in one particle is simultaneously duplicated by the other (as stated by Bell's Theorem), does this imply that the connection between them may also join you and me? Must I "know" you in order to have this connection? If there is a connection, does that connection carry obligations or responsibilities?

Does quantum physics provide us with a conceptual apparatus for better understanding whether there is a God? And the nature of God? If we agree there is a God, can we move beyond our childlike anthropomorphic sense of God (which involves cause and event, reward and punishment) and begin to think of God and humankind as *simultaneously* being both cause *and* event?

These questions belong as much to physics as theology; and how we frame these questions and respond to them has considerable influence on our capacity to live by intent.

Some years ago, with the cooperation of the editors of *The New York Times*, a researcher obtained the Sunday *New York Times* crossword puzzle early on a Saturday morning. She had already made a random selection of nearly 1,000 adults using an established and closely supervised protocol. Each of these people met certain minimum standards. For example — all were high school graduates. But there was no information available about the level or nature of their further education, their work, discretionary income, interests or recreational pursuits. This randomly chosen group was asked to complete as much as possible of the crossword puzzle in a 30-minute period. Subjects did not know that the puzzle was still unpublished.

On Monday (following publication of the puzzle) a second group was randomly selected using the same protocol. They, too, were given 30 minutes to work on the puzzle.

The second group performed much more successfully than the first. The statistical probability of the difference not being coincidental was overwhelming.

On Saturday the selected subjects were using a puzzle which had not previously been seen. But on Sunday, following publication, several hundred thousand people found habitual pleasure in the ritual of completing *The New York Times* crossword puzzle. The Monday test group was functioning in an etheric environment which contained the energy and the accomplishments of those who had worked the puzzle on Sunday, and in some unfathomable way the Monday group was able to draw upon the acquired knowledge of the Sunday group.

This experiment has been repeated several times in the metropolitan area of New York City; and precisely the same protocol obtained virtually identical statistical results when the experiment was carried to London and *The London Times* crossword puzzle.

Let me tell you about a quite marvelous study that appeared in the *Journal of the American Medical Association* (1999). I regard it as marvelous because it is a scientifically rigorous statement of a perhaps obvious truth which many of us have accepted for years. It is an important truth and so it is good to have replicable evidence. The truth is simple enough: *When we permit ourselves to again feel significant emotional turmoil, we prepare ourselves to separate from its consequences.*

I was pleased to see that *The New York Times* devoted 40 column inches to an excellent discussion by Ms. Erica Goode of this *JAMA* article. I would like to quote from her.

> In a powerful demonstration of how intimately mind and body are linked, researchers have shown that writing about traumatic experiences measurably improves the health of some patients suffering from chronic asthma or rheumatoid arthritis.
>
> Asthma patients who wrote about "the most stressful event they had ever undergone" for 20 minutes on three consecutive days, the researchers found, showed significant improvements in lung function four months later, compared with patients who spent the same amount of time writing about emotionally neutral topics. Similarly, four months after finishing the writing exercise, rheumatoid arthritis patients presented with significantly less severity and pain.

The study, which appears in the *Journal of the American Medical Association*, is notable both for its size and its scientific rigor. It included 107 patients with moderately severe asthma or rheumatoid arthritis, and the health of the patients was monitored using objective physiological measures. Doctors who took part in the study did not know whether or not the patients they were examining had received the writing "treatment".

These findings add to increasing evidence that attention to patients' psychological needs can play an important role in the treatment of many physical illnesses, a view shared by many patients and caregivers, but one that has only recently begun to draw the attention of the medical establishment.

In an editorial accompanying the journal report, Dr. David Spiegel, professor and associate chairman of psychiatry and behavioral sciences at Stanford University, writes, "We have been closet Cartesians in modern medicine, treating the mind as though it were reactive to but otherwise disconnected from disease in the body".

The patients in the "treatment" group were instructed to write down their "deepest thoughts and feelings" about the traumatic experience, while control subjects wrote about their plans for the day. Subjects in both groups were instructed to write continuously for 20 minutes.

The researchers found that of the 70 patients who wrote about traumatic events, 47.1 percent showed significant improvement in their health at the end of four months, 48.6 percent showed no change and 4.3 percent got worse. In the control group, 24.3 percent showed improvement, 54.1 percent showed no change and 21.6 percent got worse.

At first blush, this is remarkable. The "treatment" consisted of just 20 minutes of writing on three consecutive days. But four months after receiving this "therapy", nearly half of the chronically ill writers showed significant improvement in their well-being. Notice, also, that this significant improvement did not involve pharmacology or any form of professional intercession. A common sense approach was utilized at a very high level of effectiveness. There are many, many drugs brought to market which in testing do not achieve significant improvement in nearly half of the test group.

Let me now share with you another powerful finding. It has long been known that emotions generated by personally affirming social engagement increase the activity of the brain's left frontal lobe; and those feelings that are associated with social withdrawal strengthen the response of the right frontal lobe. Dr. Tiffany Field, a psychologist at the University of Miami School of Medicine, published a stunning paper in the *Journal of Developmental Psychology* (1999).

Dr. Field and her team identified a group of new mothers who had been clinically assessed as "moderately depressed". The electrical activity of the brains of these mothers was charted and, additionally, each mother was interviewed and she also completed a standard diagnostic questionnaire. These mothers were then asked to hold their babies, whose ages ranged from three to six months, while the activity of the infant brains was charted for three minutes with a stretchable cap containing electrodes. *Remarkably, right frontal electrical brain activity substantially exceeded the left frontal regions in 13 of 17 infants of depressed mothers compared with two of 15 infants of non-depressed mothers.*

A frequent and prominent aspect of depression is "blunted affect." Those who are depressed tend to be withdrawn, uninvolved and unconnected. Typically depression is accompanied by a low level of emotional responsiveness. This is often reflected in a depressed person's scant desire for communication, verbal and non-verbal.

This study is a documentation of the extraordinary sensitivity of infants and the importance of verbal and non-verbal communication to the emotional ecology of very young children. Both of these papers support the common sense proposition that for infants, children and adults, the communication of feelings is essential.

We can regard communication as a process by which meaning is transferred. This seems straightforward enough. But when we add body language to our words and consider tone, inflection and volume, the simple transfer of meaning is quite complex.

In thinking deeply about this, we may also discover that the transfer of meaning is a process which at once requires energy while it is simultaneously altering an energy field. This perspective of communication is a linguistic equivalent to Bell's Theorem.

What is implied here is that every communication in some way alters an energy field which contains all of us. Every person on the planet. Thus — what we say and how we say it has cosmic significance.

Some of you may be aware that from time to time Transcendental Meditation Centers have selected a particular city somewhere in the world and then, without announcing the name of the city, tens of thousands of men and women would direct white light and love to that city of choice for many hours a day over a period of several days.

Biostatisticians later would study the city in question to determine whether there was any change in the frequency of violence, including vehicular accidents, during the test period.

Emergency room records were examined. The number of police and fire calls were compared with the month prior to the experiment beginning, etc. There was a close assessment of assault, rape and other examples of violence against a person.

Many of these *post hoc* examinations were conducted under an exacting protocol, and supervised by faculty from renowned universities.

More than a dozen cities throughout the world have been subjected to the power of directed transcendental meditation. *And without exception, each of these cities has shown a remarkable, statistically significant lowering of violence and hurtful behavior.*

Generally within 30 days of the meditative effort ceasing, "normal" indices of violence were reestablished. It was these experiments which first demonstrated that the synchronization of directed energy intensifies the potential for healing.

Can we offer an explanation for this phenomenon based upon the teachings of traditional science? I think not!

There are many studies in the literature which demonstrate that when a group of people synchronize their spiritual energy, there is a measurable gain in effectiveness. In the old days this was called a "prayer chain". But that phrase suggests a religious context when, in fact, I am talking about a spiritual phenomenon that may contain but goes beyond the dogma and doctrines of religion. Moreover, this is a phenomenon that can be quantified.

For example, the Princeton University scientist, Dr. Roger Nelson, has measured the statistically significant effect that focused meditations have had upon the earth's energy field. Following the death of Princess Diana, for example, subtle electromagnetic alterations were documented.

Test animals which are experimentally used to predict the advent of an earthquake also responded to the death of Princess Diana.

The transformational implications of this, individually and within the global village, are simply beyond comprehension. All of us have enormous opportunities to influence through our attitudes the quality of our own lives and the tranquility of our own communities.

This does not require a government grant or private funding or technological breakthrough. It simply calls upon us to *actively* acknowledge that within our humanness there is a spiritual energy beyond all measurement.

A favorite author, Eric Butterworth, wrote that, "God is in us, not as a raisin is in a bun, but as the ocean is in a wave." There is a resounding truth in these words which empowers any of us to be a transformational influence in the lives of every person, even the most wretched and miserable souls who share this global village with us. For us to not acknowledge this and act upon it would be a terrible waste and, indeed, would probably require us to redefine the implications and meanings of sin. Let me offer an uncomplicated example.

For at least 30 years we have had overwhelming statistical evidence that when infants are held and stroked, their mental, emotional and physical well-being is greatly advanced. Indeed, some infant studies indicate that otherwise healthy unstroked infants require nearly three years to catch up with those babies that are regularly stroked.

Knowing this, is it a sin to not actively involve one's self in bringing about a world in which all babies can be stroked? Culturally and historically we have tended to think about sin as an individual act.

But I would like to now suggest that in today's emerging world, sin has cosmic proportion and, more important, cosmic consequences.

It may be that we will learn to expand our definition of sin. Let me offer another example: If fear causes us to expect the worst possible outcome, is fear an expression of negative faith? Are we therefore committing a sin if we live in fear?

I anticipate that thoughtful people will want to affirm this broader perspective of sin and, thereby contribute to a basic reinterpretation of both religion and spirituality.

My intent in choosing the title of this chapter was heartfelt, not flip. "May the Force be with you" is a prayer, not a response to a *Trivia* question. The more each of us is able to understand the importance of this prayer, the greater is our capacity to choose a life of intent.

There is a famous story of a man condemned to death by his king. The man announces that if the king will but spare his life for a year, he will teach the king's horse to fly. The king, intrigued, grants the reprieve. When asked about this uncertain post-ponement, the man says: "Who knows? In a year's time, the king may die. The horse may die. Or maybe the damn horse will fly."

Marc Ian Barasch

Chapter XVI

SOCIAL ADAPTATION
AS A STRATEGY FOR THRIVING

Most of us understand that based on the laws of aerodynamics, the bumblebee cannot fly. The area of its wings is too small for its body mass. Of course, the bumblebee does not understand this ... and so it is able to fly quite nicely, thank you. Scientists who have studied the bumblebee tell us that it has adapted to its plight by developing extremely strong muscles where its wings meet its body. This permits a bumblebee to flap its wings with extraordinary rapidity, and so it is able to compensate for what an engineer would otherwise regard as a design flaw. However, a biologist would cite the bumblebee's wing oscillation as an example of biological adaptation. Over eons of time, the bumblebee was able to biologically adapt, and as a result of this biological adaptation in a heterogeneous environment, bumblebees gained new forms of social adaptation as well. Bumblebees created well-organized communities. They gained the ability to communicate with other bumblebees, and to live at peace in a highly functional social order.

By way of comparison, consider the plight of the brown booby whose home is on Ascension Island, an isolated Pacific Island far from the usual path of warm water currents. Generally, the water around Ascension Island is too cool to support the growth of plankton and so there are only a few fish in these waters.

This creates a serious feeding problem for the brown booby. Unlike the bumblebee, the brown booby occupies what biologists refer to as a "blind niche" in which there has been essentially no biological adaptation. The brown booby has short, stubby wings and a rather chunky body. Unlike the bumblebee, its muscle development is not remarkable. And so the brown booby can fly only a limited distance. Since the nearest island beyond Ascension is 800 miles away, a brown booby which miscalculates its ability to return home is doomed.

Most of the time brown boobies are able to marginally support their nutritional needs. Occasionally, however, meteorological conditions bring warm currents close to Ascension. Because these warm waters are rich in nutrients, plankton flourish and large numbers of fish are attracted. But this circumstance may happen only a couple of times a year.

Typically, sea birds breed on a predictable annual cycle. But the brown booby will only breed when fish are running nearby. Two weeks after mating, the female lays two eggs. While both eggs are expelled at the same time, one of them hatches precisely five days before the second. If the fish run has continued, the parents are able to feed themselves and their first-born. Then when the second egg is hatched, the parents simply push it into the sea, evidently unwilling to take on the responsibility of feeding two babies. On the other hand, if the first-born is sickly, then it is sacrificed and the second-born is supported by its parents. This phenomenon, while unusual, is not unique. There are dozens of more-or-less comparable examples in the animal world. Biologists who have studied the brown booby believe that this is a rudimentary form of adaptation which assures perpetuation of the specie despite the physical inadequacies of the bird, and a consistently difficult physical environment.

The evolutionary record demonstrates that a capacity for adaptation is an essential life force. There is a general principle at work here. *Effective biological adaptations seem to create opportunities for significant social adaptation.* During ordinary times all animals, including humans, can rely on established patterns of social adaptation. But during extraordinary times, the pace of social adaptation must be accelerated.

Among the higher animals, social adaptation often becomes more important than biological adaptation. That's why Dr. Jonas Salk said, "The principle of survival of the fittest is being displaced by the principle of survival of the wisest." By "survival of the fittest" I believe that Salk is referring to biological adaptation. But "survival of the wisest" is a clear example of social adaptation. Surely we can agree that the magnitude of change which we are enduring, and its rapidity and unpredictability, challenge us to open ourselves to new forms of social adaptation. We can become wiser.

If the pioneers who settled the midwest had lived in London, England, they would not have created the custom of barn-raising. The vastness of the midwest and the sparse population required a new social adaptation. As social adaptations are refined, they tend to develop a ceremonial structure which then helps newcomers to know how to behave. Ceremony becomes a way for the community to express its collective expectations.

Cultural anthropologists and sociologists seek to understand a culture by studying its ceremonies and related symbology. That was the intent of Charles Reich when some years ago he developed a theory which identified three stages of American consciousness. Later Paul Gardner, in his book, *Nice Guys Finish Last: Sport and American Life*, applied Reich's theory to sports where he found cultural meaning in the organizational dynamic of the dominant sport.

According to Gardner, baseball is the sport of Consciousness I, which had its origin in 19th century, small town rural America. Gardner reminds us that there is a unique quality of leisure about baseball. It is the only national sport which is not time-based. Baseball is a game which requires inter-independence; very much on the model of the small town. And baseball is a game which requires a curious blend of intuition, statistical analysis and strategic thinking.

He argues that this is the same mindset which assures success in virtually all expressions of rural and small town economics. He even suggests that the manager of the baseball team and the pastor of the church both require this mindset, and the absence of it assures a loss of effectiveness for either person.

Football is the sport of Consciousness II. It is a sport which requires a high degree of specialization of function. Like the factory, it openly utilizes hierarchy. Unlike baseball, where strategies are spontaneous, football is based on carefully devised formulations, or "plays", which are practiced over and over again. Football generally requires players of unusual strength and size; in this sense it is a highly "industrial" game. (In the industrial era, men who were physically slight or weak did not work in steel mills.)

Football introduces the concept that "winning is everything", an idea which became a cultural imperative in industrial capitalism. During this industrial era, civil service demonstrated that the name and personality of an office typist was irrelevant. What mattered was that we hired a Class Three typist, which assured us that she had at least two, but no more than five years of experience, and that she could type at least 45 words per minute. Similarly, football emphasizes performance, not personality, and in the presence of good numbers, deviant personal behaviors are tolerated.

Gardner's book was written in the early 1970s. But even then he wondered if basketball would become the sport of Consciousness III. He talked about a sport which values skill over force, flow over formalization, and improvisation over planning. He described how in basketball the human body is more nearly in its natural form rather than heavily armored.

Above all, basketball encourages each player, not just the quarterback or pitcher, to accept personal responsibility for team outcome. Because basketball can be described as a "flow sport" and there are only five players on a team, each player is expected to develop a high level of skill in every aspect of the sport. The idea of "specialization" is broadly horizontal rather than narrow and vertical.

It's interesting to me that at virtually every basketball game, there are a large number of celebrities in attendance. My sense is that basketball attracts many more trendsetters than either football or baseball. Somehow trendsetters seem to innately realize that basketball is the preferred cultural metaphor. This is easy to demonstrate. Consider the corporations in America which are most widely admired and ask yourself which of these three sports provides the most admired organizational model.

Often what appear to be localized examples of social adaptation and invention find expression in other places and activities. That is why the history of ideas is so fascinating. More than that, I am struck by how people from different cultures and with radically different life experiences create ideas independent of each other which, nonetheless, seem to have a shared cosmic purpose.

How curious it is that Columbus took his famous voyages at almost precisely the same time John Gutenberg invented moveable type. By reason of his discoveries, Columbus dispelled the notion of the flat earth, and thereby corrected the theological arrogance of the Church. Because of Columbus, a calculus of social, political and economic events were put into motion. And as a result of Gutenberg's invention, the human mind was similarly expanded. In just three years, the number of books in Europe increased from less than 500 to more than 10,000. Ten years later, there were three million books in Europe. It may be that through his invention, John Gutenberg is responsible, directly and indirectly, for a proliferation of knowledge that was not surpassed until the development of the personal computer.

New ideas seem to contribute to the creation of other new ideas. Sometimes this synergistic process is clear and direct. Or we may have to wait for years before we can see and appreciate the importance of the connection. Here's an illustration from American history.

Bessemer taught us a new way to make large quantities of steel, quickly and inexpensively. This soon encouraged the development of rolling mills, and then we quickly learned to make "I" beams which, in turn, permitted architects to develop a new concept — the skyscraper. While the "I" beam allowed construction, the skyscraper was not a feasible concept until we learned to weave steel into cable, thus allowing a new mode of vertical travel — elevators.

At about the same time we realized that with only minor adaptation, "I" beams could become rails. Without rails, there could not have been railroads. And without railroads, the social, political and economic history of this nation (and the world) would have been dramatically different. Looking backward the flow of these connections is clear. But when the Bessemer furnace was first introduced, it would have been difficult to appreciate how it would l ead to the many gigantic consequences of the "westward ho" movement.

How can it be that at about the same time that Picasso was experimenting with cubism (which permits us to simultaneously see several different perspectives of the same object), physicists were abandoning the idea of a fixed physical reality, telling us that atoms could at once be seen as both particles and waves. And when we learned that merely by observing the behavior of atoms, we cause them to behave differently, we changed forever our perception of what (in the words of my son Adam) is "really real".

Suddenly the apparently simple matter of physical reality raised profound metaphysical questions, not only about reality but also about the scientist's demi-god, objectivity. While all this was going on, classically trained composers were "inventing" a-tonal forms of musical expression that represented a new dismantling of old models and established traditions in a process that might be described as "aural cubism".

As I read history, these "coincidences" and connections have always been with us…although sometimes it has taken us a generation or two to appreciate the process. Perhaps you would like to attribute this never-ending profusion of related events to serendipity. But that is not comfortable for me. There are many other explanations which for me make more sense: The phenomenon of the nonlocal mind; Jung's concept of a collective unconscious; and Rupert Sheldrake's work on morphic resonance seem more to the point. At least from my perspective.

My purpose is not to advance an explanation of the "coincidences" which occur throughout recorded history. Instead I ask you to consider the apparent coincidences which are evident today…and then to ask yourself what they might mean. My family had a young lady from Sweden living with us as an exchange student. While I realize that it's hardly remarkable, it still is a bit amazing to my antiquarian mind that she can send an e-mail letter to her brother in Sweden which he instantly receives.

There is no doubt we will soon have more and more efficient ways of searching the Internet. Anyone who spends even a few hours "surfing" must be overwhelmed by the extraordinary array of information which is accessible.

Recently I was "hip deep" in a research project which required me to use several different databases. My sense is that it's virtually impossible to imagine wanting information that is not readily available…if only you know where to look. Clearly — new social adaptations are being formed at a furious pace. For example — the virtual office, home businesses and the phenomenon of the stand-alone consultant. Work is no longer defined by a location, established hours or prescribed tasks. One person, working alone, can uncover a limitless array of information that ten years ago was beyond the collective reach of a workforce of 10,000.

Major social adaptations often seem to form a constellation of behaviors around a primary theme. Consider with me the broad sweep of economics over the past 250 years. During the agricultural era, the basic economic asset was land.

Clearly a finite asset. Money was the basic economic asset of the industrial era. Less limited. But still finite. The basic economic asset today is knowledge.

This is the first time in the history of the world when the basic economic asset is non-depletable, infinitely reusable and totally regenerative. Every time we use knowledge, we create more of it. While this is certainly not a new insight, I do not believe that it is yet culturally understood or appreciated. The value of a patent is today much different, and much less, than 20 years ago. The Federal Reserve system and the central banks of other nations perpetuate the myth that their 19th century monetary techniques allow them to willfully influence the rate of interest and the velocity of money. Drucker and others have written about the "borderless nation". The ability to move billions of dollars from anywhere to anywhere with a few keystrokes irrevocably alters the world.

Of course, old ways are slow to change. As a case in point, when American companies export CD software, for many years government statisticians calculate the value of the exported goods as equal to the cost of the packaging plus the cost of the vinyl (approximately 1.3 cents per pound). The market value of the software is ignored. Here's a question for you to ponder. Would you rather own a manufacturing line in a GM plant? Or have Bill Gates sitting under a pine tree, designing, while you hold an exclusive contract on his creative output?

Probably you have heard the economic cliché, "Money goes where it's best treated." This means that the flow of money follows the rate of interest. And if we are talking a billion dollars, then one-tenth of one percent is a lot of money. Simple logic tells us that those nations, or corporations, which most need money will attract it by raising the rate of interest. This ebb and flow is on-going, 24 hours a day, seven days a week. There are many, many ramifications to this.

While not everyone agrees with me, I believe that this phenomenon virtually assures a flattening of the business cycle. Deep inflation/deflation is much less possible. And the flattened cycle will be completed in a much briefer time. The ability of workers to move from nation to nation in Europe, freely and without the permission of any government, radically changes what we mean by a workforce.

We are rapidly approaching the day when virtually all of the world will be organized into only a few trading alliances, and with the dominance of these alliances we will ultimately see the end of tariffs. The economics of any single nation is becoming an obsolete concept. It's like having a major nuclear accident in Russia and bureaucratically requiring the fallout to not cross the border.

If knowledge is the basic economic asset of today's economy, then why have I been discussing money in such detail? After all, money was the basic economic asset of the earlier industrial era. The reason is subtle. But simple. And very, very important. During the industrial era, money was the object...the desired outcome. As a generalization, whatever we did during the industrial era was done to make money. Yes, there may have been some secondary (and even altruistic) benefits. But the primary intent of all industrial era activities was to generate money in the form of profit.

Today, however, profit cannot be the primary corporate objective. Today the generation and utilization of knowledge must be the primary objective. *Money becomes a consequence of knowledge or an outcome of it. It is a representation of the value which is placed on knowledge. But it is not the purpose of an enterprise.* Often in my work with clients, we must deal with a fundamental confusion about this distinction.

Recently I spent several hours with a client. His avowed intent is to help people enhance their wellbeing. But his attitude toward money, and the attitude of his staff toward money, have caused them to create systems which communicate to their clients that the primary objective of their business *is* to make money. It is my belief that if he and his staff can learn to fully invest themselves in the enhancement of clients' wellbeing, money will follow. Easily. Comfortably. Bountifully. In today's era, dollars follow attitudes, not business plans.

Let me say this another way. In the old model, and in this client's office, I sense a shame-based, rigid, perhaps even a punitive attitude toward money. It is my belief that in today's culture when through our work we are able to create joy in people's lives, their response is joy-filled. The payment of a fee is an expression of gratitude. They are paying us with "happy dollars".

My client lives and works within a cosmic environment which is rapidly changing. But his capacity for accommodation has not yet permitted him to act congruently within that environment. His challenge is our challenge. If we are to thrive, personally and in our own businesses, we must learn to ask, "Why?" rather than, "How?" Redefining ourselves and redefining our businesses is one process, not two. *Where role was once admired, authenticity is now required.* Our finest opportunity for economic success is in becoming more fully who we are.

Come, come, whoever you are —
wanderer, worshiper, lover. It doesn't
matter. Ours is not a caravan of
despair. Come, even if you have
broken your vow a thousand times.
Come, come yet again, come.

Inscription on the tomb of
Jelaluddin Rumi,
12th century Iranian poet

Chapter XVII

SOME CORE BELIEFS ABOUT HELPING OTHERS

The pages you are now holding represent a philosophy, a set of principles and an inner-directed process that over the years I've referred to as "living by intent". This phrase is a brief form which hopefully represents the content of *Choosing to Choose*.

The incubation of this book has been underway for many years. In preparing myself to write *Choosing to Choose*, I've drawn freely from the wisdom literature of the world. Should you find some worthy ideas in my book, please take them and know they are yours. Neither attribution nor gratitude is necessary (although attribution will certainly be appreciated). Every idea that is known (by me or anyone) was known before and will always be known. You would not be taking from me; you would be claiming what is yours.

As you read this final chapter, you have reached an end. But within every ending there is a beginning. It's important to remember that while living by intent is counter-cultural, *nonetheless it is a way of life that is thoroughly natural.* There's nothing new to learn; we need only to unlearn some old attitudes and thereby release our inner potential.

The benefits of living by intent are not easily circumscribed. But surely they would include an abiding sense of abundance . . . personal empowerment . . . free access to the limitless spiritual energy that is within all of us . . . the white light of creativity . . . mobilization of our innate capacity for healing . . . and the restoration or amplification of peace and wholeness, nobility and purpose.

The way is simple. Not easy. But simple. It is freely available to you without dollar cost — though you will pay a fee in other coin. The processes of living by intent will assure you a channel of personal service that authentically reflects your own inner beauty. Through it all — even as you are burning bridges and busting old paradigms — I promise you will be having fun!

This chapter provides an overview of how I have internalized the philosophy and principles of living by intent; and how I've represented these beliefs in my work. I am clear that the path I have followed is not the only path; and it need not be your path. I feel justified in offering you this chapter because it completes a circle.

Each of us who aspires to help others must learn how to implement the philosophy and principles of living by intent. The word "how" implies tactics and techniques.

These are essential outer reality considerations. But they are valid only as an extension of inner reality philosophy and principles. (Here is another example of inside/out.)

I recognize there are some severe limitations to what I have done. A long essay, perhaps even a book, could probably be written about each of my briefly stated beliefs. And, of course, the listing is not complete. If you chose to do so, I suspect you could easily extract from my book a hundred or more additional core beliefs.

But there is an important benefit. Because you are now familiar with my book, you can place my core beliefs within a context; and that permits you to see the interplay between "why" and "what" and "how". Your observation of how my beliefs have evolved will support and facilitate your own evolution. Please understand that I offer you this chapter as a personal statement. I do not imply that these should be your core beliefs. But I invite you to take any of them from the pages that follow and, as you think is appropriate, adapt them to your hand and heart.

I wish you well.

○ ○ ○

1. When two people communicate, openly and freely, without imposing expectations or judgments on each other, their conversation has life-changing potential. They are helping each other to become more fully who they really are. Authenticity emerges. Whenever we are able to do this, we are contributing to personal growth. The challenge is to avoid implying a judgment or imposing an expectation. Of course, for this to happen, each of us must be willing to step out of our accustomed role and let ourselves be vulnerable.

2. As a helper and facilitator, I am responsible for establishing a climate in which helping can occur. There are at least three important aspects to this climate. I must have the ability and willingness to be real and genuine. No pretense or make-believe. No game-playing. The second attribute involves my ability and willingness to care for the other person and to wholly accept that person — without condition. The third attribute is empathy, meaning my ability and willingness to receive the feelings of another person, especially how the other person is then experiencing the world.

   When I am able to establish and maintain this helping climate, over a period of time a client will reflect this climate and contribute to it. As we become mutually comfortable with this process, there is high potential for personal growth and empowerment. This is a magical time during which my client and I are deriving benefits from reciprocal learning.

3. During these magical times, *my* function is to facilitate a client's clarity and intent so that s/he can make good choices. But responsibility for those choices *always* belongs to the client.

4. A "good choice" is not a moral judgment. A good choice reflects, without distortion, a client's most cherished aspirations, beliefs and desires. As these become more clear we share responsibility for developing a plan that will support a client's attainment of a life of choice.

5. I believe each of us has an inner awareness of our most pure and noble self and our highest aspirations. Even when we cannot access this awareness, it is nonetheless within each of us. I also believe that each of us knows (or we can discover) a unique channel of service that authentically reflects who we are and what we cherish. Finding and responding to that channel of service is the essence of personal empowerment.

6. My perspective is phenomenological. This is a big word which simply means that I place primary emphasis on a client's here-and-now feelings. I focus upon a client's current experiences and the contextual meanings which s/he places on those experiences. I am less concerned with the origin of those feelings and meanings.

7. My attitudes are existential. Thus, I believe that psychologically and spiritually, love is the highest goal to which any of us can aspire. Even as we learn to reach out in love, we are aware of the pain of loneliness. The pull-and-tug between our desire for love and our innate awareness of loneliness is a primal source of anxiety.

8 I believe we always have choices; and that we are simultaneously free to make choices, which is what freedom is all about, and to accept responsibility for those choices. The pull-and-tug between freedom and responsibility is an especially valuable gift. Because of this gift, we have continuing opportunity to redefine ourselves.

9. In order to think significantly about life, it is first necessary to think deeply about death. Not simply as an abstraction but also as an affirmation and acceptance of our own mortality.

10. If we are to realize our potential, I believe that issues of incomplete grieving and incomplete forgiveness must be *collegially* addressed. This is a crucial process that calls for a high level of trust, gentleness and respect.

11. We cannot change events in our past. But we can change our perception of these events. In this way, I believe we can free ourselves from the bondage of the past and prepare ourselves for a future of choice.

12. For all of these reasons, I believe that each client's sense of reality is unique, personal and, therefore, purely subjective. *There is no objective reality.* A client's beliefs and experiences are what is important; *and those beliefs and experiences need to be understood within the context of the client's life.* All experiences and feelings — even those which a person may not yet recognize or doesn't want to claim — have meaning and purpose. My task is to *appreciate* these beliefs and to acknowledge a client's feelings about his/her experiences. Beliefs and experiences had meaning at the time of their origin; and they have meaning now.

13. I believe my commitment to a client must be holistic. It is not useful to explore this or that splinter of a client's life as though it is separate and distinct. It isn't. There is no dynamic meaning except in the totality of a client's life.

14. By extension, I believe a client's life must first be appreciated and later understood within a social context. Until I am able to truly appreciate an individual within the context of family, friends and associates, I cannot be helpful.

15. I believe a primary function of the past is to help all of us become more clear about those feelings which we would like to *not* have. By understanding the past in terms of the feelings which we do *not* enjoy, we prepare ourselves to design a future that assures a greater measure of the feelings we do enjoy.

16. I believe a client and I have a shared responsibility for identifying the "mental models" of his/her life. [Mental models are the unseen, ill-defined assumptions which are inevitably operative in our lives — but rarely considered.] I have observed over and over again that these unseen assumptions are represented in choices, conscious and unconscious. A client's choices contribute importantly to his/her behaviors which, in turn, influence the conduct of a client's life. This process is on-going and from time-to-time there may be self-discovered realization that some behaviors are in conflict with the purity of a client's aspirations. When a client is able to emotionally own these conflicts, s/he can begin to move beyond feelings of vulnerability, inferiority and inadequacy and toward feelings of confidence and mastery.

17. I believe that personal effectiveness requires a highly developed sense of belonging. Unconditional acceptance is a non-negotiable requirement of deep belonging, and deep belonging points a client toward mastery. Feelings of inferiority are related to an inadequate sense of belonging. Thus, happiness and a sense of belonging are importantly linked. Feelings of security and acceptance are similarly derived from the quality of belonging.

18. A feeling of being "belonged" is first experienced by the infant. But it is a continuing part of everyone's developmental cycle — literally from birth to death. It is this feeling of belonging which allows us to establish the social connections that grow into community.

I've come to believe that intense anxiety is often visible evidence of inadequate social connection. Should these visible symptoms be part of a client's behavior, together we may also find that the client will have developed an elaborate private logic to explain and justify these feelings of deprivation. There is a temptation to focus on this private logic. But in my experience, it is much more productive to help a client develop a more satisfying social context. As this happens, private logic is displaced by a new level of social connection, and so a client will have more confidence in his/her own inner identify and, therefore, less need for the protection of a shield of anxiety.

19. I believe that my work with a client *must* be marked by collaboration. An implied hierarchy between us negates the possibility of success. A client cannot be a passive recipient in the process. The client must accept responsibility to be an active participant in a relationship of equality.

20. I believe each of us is born with a special meaning for our lives, and that, all of us who strive for maturity, joy and service are obliged to discover the themes of our own life drama. The existential challenge is for me and my client to be concerned with issues of Being rather than involving ourselves with a never-ending process of problem-solving. Issues of Being (as I understand them) include intimacy, sexuality, aging, grieving, death and, often, the resolution of primal relationships — sometimes with people who have been long deceased.

21. Viktor Frankl suggested that while we usually have the means to live, often we have no meaning to live for. I believe many people have an unrecognized or unacknowledged fear that upon death their lives will be judged to have had no meaning. I observe that this fear tends to become more acute as we grow older and/or our personal relationships are tattered. I recognize, of course, that this is a classic existential dilemma. My *strong belief is that meaninglessness cannot be addressed through Doing. It is an issue of Being.* I find great joy in helping a person to understand this.

22. Over the years, I've learned that I cannot work effectively with a person who defines him/herself as "sick". A person may be sick of the quality of life s/he has been enduring. A person may be sick of being sick. A person may feel shame at his/her inability to master the processes of living. *But these attitudes and others like them do not constitute sickness unless a person has also defined him/herself as a helpless, hopeless victim.*

23. *Anxiety is inherent to life and so, therefore, it is natural.* But culturally many people endure an extraordinarily heavy burden of anxiety that goes far, far beyond what is natural. For this reason, it is not surprising that issues of alienation and fragmentation are important to so many of us. These issues are often a symptom of a Being disorder; and so it is important that I help a client to separate the symptom from the problem. Together our challenge is to enrich quality of Being rather than attempting to directly address the symptoms or etiology of anxiety.

24. I believe existential anxiety *always* involves a consciousness of our own freedom. (An important cause of anxiety is the chronically inadequate use of our freedom.) All of us have been free (and are free) to invest ourselves in ways that do *not* provide us with an adequate sense of belonging. Each of us must recognize our responsibility for this situation; and, regardless of age or circumstance, we can then participate in our own healing. This process of healing *always* involves other people with whom we feel profound trust. It cannot be done alone and, ultimately, it cannot be done without learning to acknowledge our feelings and resonate with them. Thus — in a client relationship, trust is the single most important point of connection.

Trust is an outcome, not an event or a state of being. First — a client must feel listened to. Second — a client must feel heard. More than heard, a client must also feel understood. Finally — when a client feels unconditionally accepted by me — then s/he is able to permit feelings of vulnerability. At that moment — and not before — trust becomes an available resource.

25. I believe if we choose to *not* choose, we create a situation in which feelings of inadequacy and guilt are inevitable. Sartre said *"We are our choices"*. Whether it is deliberate or not, if a client has chosen an inauthentic mode of existence, I believe personal responsibility for life issues are being ignored and, perhaps even more serious, a client is passively assuming that existence is mostly controlled by external forces. My task, then, is to facilitate a client's understanding that freedom and responsibility are inseparable, *and that the locus of control is within the individual.*

26. As I have acknowledged elsewhere, I developed the idea of intentionality from the work of Paul Tillich. Living by intent is an inside/out phenomenon. I observe that from time to time a person will have a profound fear that s/he has no meaningful core . . . no internalized substance . . . no self. It is as though this person is saying, "There is really nothing to me. I'm an empty shell. I'm hollow." Clearly, in this circumstance it would be inappropriate to explore the idea of living by intent. But I observe that when a person has feelings of unworthiness, there is usually a spiritual void. Well-being *requires* an awareness of self as part of a cosmic whole.

27. "Why am I here? What do I want from life? What will give my life purpose? What is the source of meaning in my life? When my life has ended, will I be remembered? And will those remembrances relate to deep meaning?" When a client chooses to work with me, it would be unusual for him/her to immedi-

ately find *personal* relevance in these questions. But my observation is that these questions are universally relevant. *It is essential that I begin wherever the client is. It might take a year or more for us to move through a client's concrete concerns so that we can then address underlying issues — including existential anxiety.*

28. I believe that feelings of existential anxiety deplete meaningful creativity. Here's why. A component of anxiety is fear. The fear associated with anxiety is deep, generalized and undifferentiated. Creativity requires risk. In the presence of fear, it is too risky to risk and so creativity is stifled. When issues of anxiety are resolved, there is a tremendous surge of creative energy. I cannot over-emphasize the benefits to an individual who is freely able to access the wellspring of his/her creativity.

29. I believe it is *never* appropriate for me to judge whether a client is living authentically. But should a client self-discover areas of inauthenticity, it is appropriate for me to help a client to become a more centered Being. Generally this involves helping him/her to make better choices about the utilization of "natural resources". [By natural resources, I am referring to each person's use of his/her time, energy, gifts, opportunities and money.] It is not necessary for a client to learn to grow. *Growth is natural.* If growth is not occurring in some aspect of life, we can postulate the presence of artificial constraints. Removal of these constraints permits the natural process of growth to rejuvenate.

30. A challenge which all of us share is the painful task of self-discovering the ways in which our personal identities have been determined by others. This brings us face-to-face with the realization that most

of our lives we have been seeking from others both approval and confirmation of our Being.

When we become free to choose, our choices are more and more Being-centered. This better permits us to establish meaningful channels of altruistic service, and so we are able to evolve a deeper sense of belonging. As feelings of belonging are intensified, so also are our feelings of being "belonged". The security of belonging and being belonged allows us to more effectively confront existential anxieties and, thereby, we become more free, more creative, more productive.

Please let me end this chapter by offering a gift — these beautiful words by Nelson Mandela:

"Our deepest fear is not that we are inadequate. Our deepest fear is that we are powerful beyond measure. It is our light, not our darkness, that frightens us. We ask ourselves, 'Who am I to be brilliant, gorgeous, talented, fabulous?' Actually, who are you not to be? You are a child of God. Your playing small does not serve the world. There is nothing enlightened about shrinking so that other people won't feel insecure around us. We are born to make manifest the glory that is within us. It is not just in some of us. It is in everyone. And as we let our own light shine, we unconsciously give other people permission to do the same. When we are liberated from our own fears, our presence automatically liberates others."

Rabbi Zusya of Hanipol used to say, "If they ask me in the next world, 'Why were you not more like Moses?' I will know the answer. But if they ask me, 'Why were you not more like Zusya?' I will have nothing to say."

Martin Buber

AN AFTERWORD
TO THE SECOND EDITION

Everyone knows that in 1999 a sheep named Dolly was successfully cloned by English scientist from a single cell taken from the teat of her "mother". At the time Dolly's birth was announced, scientists were emphasizing the enormous gulf between cloning a sheep and cloning a human.

But only months after Dolly's birth, Oregon genetic scientists had successfully cloned a Rhesus monkey. The essential proteins of this small primate are 97% shared with you and me, and so cloning a Rhesus monkey demonstrates that the technology for human cloning is close at hand. When I scan the world literature, it is clear that literally hundreds of groups are now refining the technique for cloning humans. As a futurist, who is now privileged to witness the unfolding of the 21st century, I'm confident that the successful cloning of a human is imminent. Perhaps in a few months. Certainly within a few years.

Scientists are learning how to tinker with DNA. Indeed, it is now possible to literally turn on (or turn off) several specific genetic switches which govern various aspects of embryo development. Here is a bizarre example:

A group of scientists in England have learned to hatch headless minnows. I'm confident the day will come when scientists will have the ability to produce headless human infants. I am already finding justification for this possibility in the writings of some scientists. For example — might we someday produce cloned human creatures that have no head and are solely intended to provide a "parts inventory" for those of us who do have heads but, as a result of trauma or aging, discover that a body part or two needs replacement? Clearly, even a hypothetical discussion of this possibility raises critical questions about what is life and what are the meanings of life. Should we consider a purposefully-bred infant with no head as human? Is there a soul? Does this headless child have one? How would you feel about accepting an organ from a head-less baby in behalf of a loved one who otherwise was confronting certain death?

I am not angry with the scientists who are doing this work. They are fulfilling their function — seeking basic knowledge. A knife is not moral or immoral; it derives its morality from the hand of the user. Similarly, pure knowledge is also amoral. How we choose to apply that knowledge may raise profoundly moral questions. But these questions involve the application of knowledge and are not intrinsic to knowledge itself or the process of discovery. I'm reminded of the words written by Ayn Rand: "The first man to have discovered fire was no doubt burned at the stake."

The issue here is not new. It has followed us through all of recorded history. At every time and at every place, questions of morality have always been stimulated by achievements in science and technology. During the early days of the Industrial Revolution in England, the Luddites argued that steam-driven machinery was immoral. Indeed — these well-intentioned, fearful men and women looked upon machine technology as an invention of the devil.

It is virtually certain that regardless of how you earn your living, you are now confronting change of enormous magnitude. That's why some years ago Peter Drucker told his readers that a successful business enterprise will need to redefine its basic business about every ten years. Of course, the redefinition of a business *first* requires the generation of a vision.

All transformational ideas emerge from a transformational vision. And a transformational vision always begins in the heart and head of one person. At least initially, the vision is not understood or appreciated by more than a few compatriots. When implementation of a transformational vision begins, it always causes disjoint experiences for those who are touched by it.

This truth has long been with us. And the counter-cultural implications of this truth have always produced great stress. For example — when steam locomotives were displaced by electric locomotives, firemen continued to ride in the cab for 30 years although they had no coal to shovel. This and similar examples are familiar to all of us. But we are living during a time of transformational change and so there are many other, often more subtle examples.

Perhaps your work seems less eventful or public than creating headless minnows. But your life and your activities are no less important. Many of us are parents and grandparents. In the ordinary moments of our lives, we make decisions which, in exquisite and subtle ways, contribute to the attitudes, beliefs and values of our children and our children's children.

In this way, we are importantly influencing their life choices — including the choice of a mate — and, thereby, we are influencing the lives of children who will not be conceived for another generation and beyond. In the 19th century, we recognized The Great Chain of Being; it's time for us to again remember that we are still part of a continuum without end. Through our authentic exercise of autonomy and freedom, personally *and* in our work, we are able to help our children and grandchildren become more fully free and freely autonomous.

The inner reality of living by intent and the outer reality manifestations of it are best seen on a daily basis through our work. I know no better statement of this relationship than these words by E. F. Schumacher:

> Considering the centrality of work in human life, one might expect that every textbook on economics, sociology, politics and related subjects would present a theory of work as one of the indispensable foundation stones for all further expositions. After all, it is work which occupies most of the energies of the human race, and what people actually do is generally deemed more important for understanding them than what they say or how they spend their money or their vote. *A person's work is deeply related to character and personality*. But the truth of the

matter is that we look in vain for a meaningful under-standing of work in all of the textbooks.

The question of what work does to the worker is hardly ever asked, not to mention the question of whether the real task might not be to adapt work to the needs of the worker rather than to demand that the worker adapt himself to the needs of the work. *Let us ask then: How does work relate to the end of purpose of being?*

It has been recognized in all authentic teachings of mankind that every human being born into this world has an opportunity to work not merely for physical sustenance, but also to strive toward transcendent excellence. How and why this happens is what I mean by the proper study of work.

Many of you have been friends and clients for a number of years. And so you are already aware that the work of E. F. Schumacher has greatly influenced my perception of the world. Today I want to mention two small volumes. I was introduced to Schumacher's ideas through his first and justly famous book, *Small is Beautiful*. His perspective of "human scale technology" (which was radical when he first expressed it) is now a major cultural trend that is at the very core of the world-wide environmental movement. This book wonderfully demonstrates the power of ideas.

Thirty years ago, when this book first appeared, it would have been difficult to imagine the influence it would have. But today we can appreciate how Shumacher's ideas have been profoundly germinal. It's hard to imagine our recent social history without the benefit of Schumacher's perspective. Over the next generation, I confidently predict that *Small is Beautiful* will still be used as a fulcrum for levers of many minds.

Two years after Schumacher's sad and early death, a compilation of several of his lectures appeared under the title of *Good Work*. This little book is not easy to find. But it is well worth the effort. Here is where Schumacher identifies the three purposes of human work.

> *First* — to provide necessary and useful goods and services.
>
> *Second* — to enable each of us to be a good steward in the use and development of our gifts.
>
> *Third* — to cooperatively do this in service to others so that through altruism we are able to liberate ourselves from our egocentricities and, thereby, more fully realize our own inherent spiritual energy.

The first of these purposes is straightforward. In many ways, Schumacher was an austere and disciplined fellow. I've always sensed a sternness in him that has been a bit uncomfortable for me. "Necessary" and "useful" are good words but much in life that brings joy and meaning might also be described as "desirable" and so I wish that his statement of the first purpose had been a bit more expansive.

I am enchanted by his second statement of purpose. *He is saying that all work which is satisfactory must also be satisfying. And even more — that work cannot be satisfying unless it contributes to a worker's personal growth.* This is an extraordinary, powerful idea that has appeared from time to time in the world's 10,000 year wisdom literature. Surely we can agree that a commitment to live by intent *must* include work that is personally satisfying. But in stating his third purpose, Schumacher is telling us that the purpose of work goes beyond the economic requirements of life. Through work that serves a greater good, each of us has an opportunity to more fully realize the inherent power and energy of our spiritual being. The outcome of personal empowerment is service, not selfishness.

If you care to think deeply about Schumacher's words, it seems to me that he is also offering us a perspective of risk. From time to time a client will tell me, "I'm a risk-adverse person." And then I will ask, "Are you a growth-adverse person as well?" The purpose of my question is to illustrate that growth inevitably involves change; *and change always entails risk.*

There are rich, life-centering implications to this. For example — Schumacher's idea of work causes us to think about how we might define "security". When we perceive work as having a spiritual core, does this perception influence the meaning we assign to "security"? In today's terms, how does work influence the ecology of the mind and the soul ... or is ecology to be confined to the wetlands and the rain forests? I submit that these are fit and proper questions to ask ourselves as we move toward attaining a life of intent.

Risk-adversity (or growth-adversity) predictably influences an individual. Surely we can agree that a risk-adverse person tends to not be spontaneous and, therefore, cannot easily live in the here-and-now moment. Similarly, the risk-adverse person tends to not be willing to explore new ideas and experiences. Perhaps we might describe this person as rigid and/or compulsive. *If you will accept the commonsense logic of these observations, then does it not follow that this path leads away from the opportunities of intentional living?*

Here is a good place to share a favorite quotation. The author is Alfred North Whitehead, the esteemed American philosopher and mathematician. "It is the business of the future to be dangerous." I believe he is telling us that "It is the business of the future to be different than what we have known." The danger lies in the unknown. But without the unknown, there is only the sameness of no-growth.

One more observation. Those who see themselves as risk-adverse are inclined to create a cognitive justification for their attitudes. But in my experience, beneath these intellectualized attitudes is fear. I love these words by Marianne Williamson: "Darkness is merely the absence of light, and fear is merely the absence of love." We might ask, "Love of whom?" Perhaps the answer is "love of self". Soul-satisfying, ennobling work best prospers when an individual is truly able to feel and believe that "I will be OK because I am OK."

It is my belief that I cannot know I will be OK unless I am able to freely draw upon my spiritual energy. "Soul" is a convenient abbreviation. My soul is that part of me which is a divine gift. I cannot create or destroy it. My soul is that part of me which helps me to realize that if I am less than the angels, I am infinitely more than an animal.

The fictional hero, Dr. Zhivago, tells us that "Your health is bound to be affected if, day after day, you say the opposite of what you feel, if you grovel before what you dislike and rejoice at what brings you nothing but misfortune." His words remind me of a passage in Marsha Sinetar's useful book, *Do What You Love, The Money Will Follow*. The author explains the idea of "Right Livelihood" with these lovely words. My comments are in brackets.

> The original concept of Right Livelihood is derived from the teachings of Buddha, who described it as work consciously chosen . . done with care and full awareness . . . and leading to enlightenment.
>
> *[Contemplate, please, the joy and fulfillment of Right Livelihood in your work.]*
>
> Ms. Sinetar then continues: Right Livelihood, in both its ancient and contemporary sense, embodies self-expression, commitment, mindfulness and conscious choice. Finding and doing this sort of work is predicated upon high self-esteem and self-trust, since only those who like themselves and who feel they are trustworthy and deserving dare to choose what is right and true for them.
>
> *[Yes! Here is the essence of personal empowerment and why personal empowerment is the seedbed of altruism.]*
>
> When you study people who are successful, as I have over the years, it is abundantly clear that their achievements are directly related to the enjoyment they derive from their work. . . . Right Livelihood is an idea about work which is linked to the natural order of things. It is doing our best at what we do best. The rewards that follow are inevitable and manifold. There is no way we can fail.

The very best way to relate to our work is to choose it. Right Livelihood is predicated on conscious choice. Unfortunately, since we learn to act upon what others say, value and expect, we often find ourselves a long way down the wrong road before realizing we did not actually choose our work.

By choosing, we learn to be responsible. We pay the price of our choices. This helps us to make better choices. Each choice we make consciously adds positively to our sense of self, and makes us trust ourselves more because we learn how to live up to our own inner standards and goals.

[She writes about "the natural order of things" and "conscious choice". She links the act of choosing to self-responsibility, and living up to "our own inner standards". It seems to me that she's offering us an illuminating view of living by intent.]

Commitment is easy when work is our Right Livelihood. *John Gardner once said the best kept secret is that people want to work hard in behalf of something that is meaningful.* As a way of working and as a way of thinking about work, Right Livelihood embodies its own psychology — a psychology of a person moving toward the fullest participation in life, a person growing in self-awareness, trust and high self-esteem. Maslow calls these people "self-actualizing". The phrase simply means growing whole. These people are life-affirming. For them, work is a way of being, an expression of love.

[The idea of "work as a way of being" instead of "work as a way of doing" is powerful!]

All people want to have transcendent values in their lives. Some may not recognize this truth … and others may be confused about how to attain and manifest transcendent values. Nonetheless — all of us (regardless of age, gender, education, economic circumstances or assigned responsibilities or privileges), knowingly or not, are walking a path in search for transcendent values.

My hope is that this book will light a candle for some who are seeking a path. There are many paths and many, many candles. If you are well-served by this candle, I am pleased.

I am convinced that all of these candles may illuminate the world in ways we cannot yet fathom. I devoutly believe this is already happening, even if we cannot always see the glow of the candles.

I am grateful to be here now.

During the time of the darkest night,
act as if morning is dawning.

Talmud

AN AFTERWORD
TO THE FIRST EDITION

The great psychoanalyst, Erik Erikson, observed that the development of an individual is not merely grounded in the past, as classic Freudian theory suggests. Erickson wrote about the "anticipated self" as a primary determinant of one's future. His observation was confirmed. Research conducted in the early days of the Headstart Program investigated the factors which seem to contribute to the success of pre-school children. *The single most important factor in predicting a pre-school child's ultimate success was the parents' image of the child's future.* One early report concluded, "Among a disadvantaged population, the best predictor variable of cognitive growth in pre-school children was the expectations of the parents."

Some 25 years ago, Benjamin D. Singer, a professor of sociology at Harvard University, was able to demonstrate that a "future-focused time perspective" was predictive of outcome among all age groups, including adults, and regardless of socio-economic variables. He initially developed and validated the idea of "future-focused role image" as a means of predicting the capacity of children and adults to move beyond their present circumstances and attain a life of choice.

But then he discovered that he could positively alter outcome when he was able to generate a future-focused role image, especially among adults. They became personally empowered, increasingly self-directed and significantly more effective as measured by peer assessment in the workplace and interpersonal family relationships. These gains encouraged the individual to achieve a new level of productivity and, thereby, an augmented sense of self-seen worthiness and esteem.

The phenomenon of future-focusing is straightforward: An individual must be able to vividly, specifically see him/herself in a future timeframe, behaving in fundamentally new ways.

Among adults, those who are able to learn to be future-focused are strongly influenced by role modeling and mentoring. Singer's data is very strong: When a person is able to project a new, vivid and specific future of choice, the probability of that future being attained is enormously enhanced.

But when a person's projection into the future is pale, blunt and uncertain, the probability of sustained and meaningful change is virtually nil.

My experience is consistent with Singer's data. Sustained and meaningful change requires a vivid, specific image of the person behaving differently in the future; *and this process is supported by affiliation with a community of similarly motivated individuals who have frequent opportunities to interact with each other and with mentors and role models.*

The most effective way to excite change within an individual is by providing opportunities for community. Sustained and meaningful change does not occur when a person works alone and is affectively isolated ... and this quality of change is not the result of reading books (even this book) or superficial, episodic and infrequent interactive experiences.

For most of us, the possibility of living a life of intent does, in fact, require us to vividly, specifically see ourselves behaving differently in a future timeframe. I know firsthand, based on my own life and the experiences of hundreds of my clients, that learning to live by intent is feasible. The process is simple because the process is natural. Simple. But not easy.

I ask you now to read again the quotation by Morris L. West which is at the beginning of this book. And having re-read it, I invite you to "reach out with both arms to the risk of living" and "embrace the world like a lover". He is correct, of course. "One has to count doubt and darkness as the cost of knowing."

But given the time in which we live, the choice to *not* act is much more serious and consequential than the risk of acting.

I wish you well. Seize *this* day for it is a beautiful day and a day of triumph.

 Avrom E. King is internationally recognized as a futurist and social psychologist. His monthly commentaries have been continually published since 1969. Within a context of emerging trends, his *Letter on Intentional Living* explores principles, processes and strategies for enhancing personal autonomy. Through his consultation practice, he facilitates the attainment of a life of choice for individuals and their organizations.